AF601728

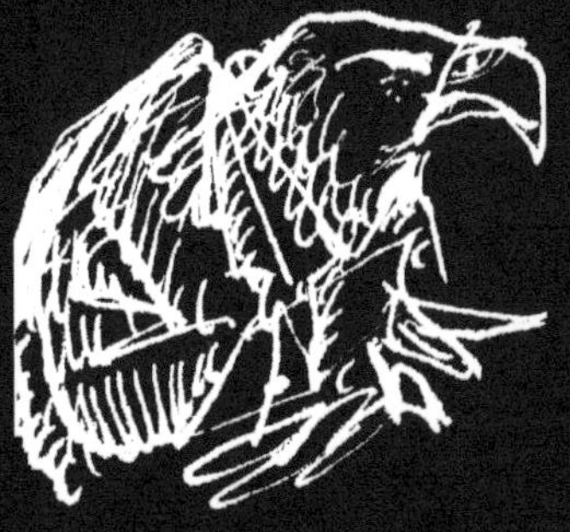

Operation Condor

Graphic design adapted from original work by Guillermo Bustamante (LOM Ediciones, Chile) and Gabriela López Introini (PRH Uruguay).

For permissions or inquiries, contact: permissions@casacarlini.com

First Edition: 2026

FRANCESCA LESSA SEBASTIÁN SANTANA

TRANSLATED FROM SPANISH BY ALEJANDRO REYES

OPERATION CONDOR

The Pact That Terrorized a Continent

TABLE of CONTENTS

To the memory of the victims of Operation Condor,
to their relatives and friends,
and to those who work constantly and tenaciously
to continue seeking truth and justice.

NOTE from AUTHORS

This book grew out of the collaboration between Francesca Lessa, an Italian researcher and international expert on Operation Condor, and Sebastián Santana, a Uruguayan-Argentine illustrator and visual artist. It is also the result of an exchange of perspectives, information, and research studies that began more than five years ago.

In 2020, Francesca saw the short film *En esta casa* (In this House), created by the Pozodeagua company with illustrations by Sebastián. The film recounts the presence of children in the clandestine detention and torture center that operated at the Defense Information Service (Servicio de Información de Defensa—SID) during Uruguay's civil-military dictatorship (1973-1985). The site, a majestic house at the corner of Artigas Boulevard and Palmar in Montevideo, has since been transformed into a site of memory, and, since 2018, houses the National Institution for Human Rights (Institución Nacional de Derechos Humanos).

In mid-2021, Francesca invited Sebastián to join a collaborative project involving the University of Oxford (where she worked until August 2023), the Sitios de Memoria Uruguay project, the Observatorio Luz Ibarburu in Uruguay, and the site of memory Londres 38 in Chile. Their goal was to create a new open-access, multilingual platform on Operation Condor.

One year later, in Buenos Aires, the website plancondor.org was launched. It collects a vast range of resources on Operation Condor and promotes the right to information for the general public, legal professionals, policy experts, scholars, survivors, and relatives. To date, the website includes:

- an interactive map of the 805 victims of the coordinated repression program that operated in South America from 1969 to 1981;
- emblematic stories of victims and the clandestine

centers where they were illegally detained;

- nearly 200 clandestine centers linked to cross-border repression, with georeferenced locati ons;
- an interactive timeline of key milestones in the history of Operation Condor and the search for truth, justice, and memory;
- criminal rulings from South American national courts and sentences from the Inter-American Court of Human Rights;
- declassified documents;
- reports and infographics on victims and trials;
- a timeline of the Rome Condor Trial;
- a dedicated section marking the 50th anniversary of Operation Condor's official founding;
- and three audiovisual pieces.

To produce the audiovisual pieces, the same team that developed *En esta casa* was reassembled: Pincho Casanova, video maker and artist; Macarena Montañez, who holds a master's in human sciences and specializes in cultural management (both directors of Pozodeagua); Sebastián; and, for this new project, musician and songwriter Diego Presa. The group worked in constant communication with Francesca. Three audiovisual pieces explore closely interconnected topics, moving from the general to the specific.

- Condor on Trial 1: Memory describes the historical and political context that led to the establishment of the military dictatorships during the Cold War, as well as the creation of Operation Condor.
- Condor on Trial 2: Justice recounts the advances and setbacks in the pursuit of justice after the democratic transitions in South America, focusing specifically on the Operation Condor trial in Argentina (1999–2018).
- Condor on Trial 3: Truth—also known as Five in Asunción—refers to the emblematic case of Argentine citizens José Luis Nell, Dora Mara Landi, Alejandro

Logoluso, and Uruguayans Gustavo Inzaurralde and Nelson Santana, who were kidnapped in Asunción, Paraguay, in March 1977 and forcibly disappeared after being secretly flown to Buenos Aires in May 1977.

After the public launch of plancondor.org, Francesca and Sebastián felt compelled to rework the images, add new ones, and adapt the texts from the audiovisual pieces into a new graph narrative in book form, first published in October 2023 in Uruguay. The first edition sold out quickly. With the approach of a double anniversary in 2025—the 50-year anniversary of the original meeting to create Operation Condor in Chile (November 1975) and the 40-year anniversary of the return of democracy in Uruguay and Brazil (March 1985)—the authors began working on a new edition of the book. In April 2025, an updated second edition was released in Uruguay; in October of the same year, a revised edition including additional cases of Chilean and Argentine victims was published in Chile.

The present English edition is published to mark the 50th anniversary in 2026 of the 1976 civil-military coup in Argentina.

We thus present this expanded and updated edition—which you now hold in your hands—with the same intention that has always guided us: to reach new audiences in hopes that they will join the essential task of preserving the memory of these events, and continue the search for truth, justice, and the unwavering demand of never again to state terrorism.

CONDOR
behind BARS

On May 27, 2016, a federal court in Buenos Aires, Argentina, sentenced 14 Argentine military officers and one from Uruguay for crimes committed during the 1970s as part of Operation Condor. The charges included kidnapping, torture, and criminal conspiracy.

Operation Condor originated from a secret agreement signed in late November 1975 during a meeting in Santiago, Chile, by the governments of Argentina, Bolivia, Chile, Paraguay, and Uruguay. Brazil joined in 1976, followed by Ecuador and Peru in 1978.

The operation enabled these South American regimes to coordinate repressive actions across borders, with the goal of eliminating political refugees living abroad. The landmark 2016 ruling in Argentina marked an important public acknowledgement: Operation Condor functioned as an illegal transnational alliance that systematically violated the human rights of political opponents exiled in South America, the United States, and Europe.

1. REVOLUTIONS *and* DICTATORSHIPS *in the* COLD WAR

After World War II ended in 1945, the victorious powers competed for global influence. On one side stood the United States and its allies; on the other, the Soviet Union and its partners. These two blocs promoted different visions of politics and economics—capitalism under American leadership, and communism alongside socialist ideals under Soviet direction.

This confrontation, known as the Cold War, began in the late 1940s and lasted until 1991. Throughout these decades, South America remained within the *sphere of influence* of the United States.

Starting in the 1950s, anti-communism became a central pillar of U.S. foreign policy, shaped by the broader struggle for world hegemony with the Soviet Union.

During this period, the United States began promoting the National Security Doctrine, a framework that would shape the ideology and actions of Latin America's armed forces and dictatorships for decades. The doctrine emphasized concepts related to the state, development, and counterinsurgency warfare, but above all, it centered on security. Achieving national security became the overriding goal, often eclipsing other concerns, including respect for human rights. The doctrine also fused anti-communist sentiment with fears of an *internal enemy*, framing the struggle as a defense of Western Christian values.

Since its founding in 1946, the United States' Western Hemisphere Institute for Security Cooperation—better known as the School of the Americas, based in Panama—has disseminated the National Security Doctrine and the concept of combating the internal enemy to more than 60,000 Latin American military and police officers.

Additionally, U.S. advisors trained police and local intelligence agents on the ground. In Uruguay, officers from the U.S. Office of Public Safety helped create and coordinate the intelligence apparatus of the Uruguayan Police, beginning in 1964.

Among those stationed there was Dan Mitrione, a U.S. police officer who promoted the use of torture and counterinsurgency techniques, training Uruguayan officers involved in the fight against the National Liberation Movement–Tupamaros.

Alongside the National Security Doctrine, the so-called French School of Counterinsurgency also arrived in South America. It brought the experience of the French military from the wars in Indochina (1946–1954) and Algeria (1954–1962), with a similar focus on the internal enemy. The tactics developed in those counter-revolutionary wars included dividing territory to control the populations, subjecting civilians to terror, and employing torture, forced disappearances, and advanced intelligence and interrogation methods. In 1957, French military officers traveled to Buenos Aires to train Argentine forces in this new form of warfare. A permanent mission of French advisors operated within the Army General Staff in Buenos Aires from 1960 to 1981.

During the Cold War, the United States and the Soviet Union never directly confronted each other militarily. But there were many indirect wars—conflicts in third countries shaped by the geopolitical and ideological context of the era—such as the Korean War (1950–1953), the Vietnam War (1954–1975), and the Cuban Missile Crisis in 1962.

Liberation movements and guerrilla organizations also emerged across the region. In South America, these included the Movement of the Revolutionary Left (MIR) in Chile (1965); the National Liberation Movement–Tupamaros (MLN-T) in Uruguay (1966); the National Liberation Army (ELN)—known as the Ñancahuazú Guerrilla—in Bolivia (1966); and the People's Revolutionary Army (ERP) in Argentina (1970).

From the mid-1960s onward, the rise of dictatorships across South America generated a broad movement of political refugees seeking safety. This circulation of militants and ideas encouraged coordinated efforts aimed at achieving a continental revolution. In 1967, both Ernesto Che Guevara and Fidel Castro supported expanding revolution throughout the Americas and promoted cooperation and solidarity among armed groups. Between 1968 and 1972, several organizations, namely the MIR in Chile, the ELN in Bolivia, the MLN-T in Uruguay, and the ERP in Argentina, began to strengthen bilateral ties. In November 1972, members of the MIR, ERP, and MLN-T met in Santiago.

There, they unanimously approved a proposal by Miguel Enríquez, leader of the MIR and host of the meeting, to unite the revolutionary vanguard against imperialist domination and create a new international organization inspired by Che Guevara's vision of establishing coordinating juntas.

A second summit took place in June 1973 in Rosario, Argentina, with larger delegations from all organizations. The ELN joined the alliance at that meeting. Finally, in mid-February 1974, representatives of the four armed groups distributed a pamphlet at a press conference in Buenos Aires. Enrique Gorriarán Merlo, a leader of the Revolutionary Workers' Party (PRT) and the People's Revolutionary Army (ERP), was among them. This pamphlet announced the creation of the Revolutionary Coordinating Junta (Junta de Coordinación Revolucionaria—JCR). The document was titled "To the Peoples of Latin America."

PARAGUAY

Date of the coup: May 4, 1954
End date: February 3, 1989
Dictator: General Alfredo Stroessner

BRAZIL

Date of the coup: March 31 and April 1, 1964
End date: March 15, 1985
Dictators: Humberto de Alencar Castelo Branco (1964–1967); Artur da Costa e Silva (1967–1969); Emílio Garrastazu Médici (1969–1974); Ernesto Geisel (1974–1979); and João Figueiredo (1979–1985)

BOLIVIA

Date of the coup: August 21, 1971
End date: July 21, 1978
Dictator: Colonel Hugo Banzer

ARGENTINA

Date of the coup: June 28, 1966
End date: May 25, 1973
Dictators: General Juan Carlos Onganía (1966–1970); General Roberto M. Levingston (1970–1971); and General Alejandro A. Lanusse (1971–1973)

URUGUAY

Date of the coup: June 27, 1973
End date: March 1, 1985
Dictators: President Juan María Bordaberry (1973–1976): Alberto Demicheli (1976); Aparicio Méndez (1976–1981); and General Gregorio Álvarez (1981–1985)

CHILE

Date of the coup: September 11, 1973
End date: March 11, 1990
Dictator: General Augusto Pinochet

2.

Since the early 1970s, and even more so after Pinochet's coup in Chile on September 11, 1973, Buenos Aires became a destination and gathering point for thousands of people. Migrants—whether for political or economic reasons—left their countries of Brazil, Paraguay, Uruguay, Bolivia, and Chile in search of safety and a new life. During those years, more than 60,000 Uruguayans lived in Argentina.

The great capital also served as a rear guard for political refugees. There, Uruguayan militants consolidated their resistance against the dictatorship back home. Buenos Aires thus became the operational headquarters for political exiles of many groups including the MLN-T, the Communist Party of Uruguay, and the Anarchist Federation of Uruguay—along with its mass wing, the Students and Workers' Resistance (Resistencia Obrero Estudiantil), and its armed wing, the Popular Revolutionary Organization–Orientals 33 (OPR-33). Given its geographical proximity to Uruguay and the ease with which militants could travel from there to Cuba or Europe whenever needed, Buenos Aires was a strategically vital location.

In addition to the Uruguayan exiles, many members of Bolivia's ELN who had fled from Chile to Argentina also gathered in Buenos Aires. Former President Juan José Torres worked to consolidate resistance against Hugo Banzer's dictatorship (1971–1978), which had overthrown his government in 1971. In 1974, militants of the MIR also established a base in Buenos Aires to reorganize the struggle against the Chilean dictatorship.

From February 27 to March 4, 1974, Argentina's Federal Police (PFA) organized a secret summit in Buenos Aires. It brought together police chiefs from Argentina, Bolivia, Chile, Paraguay, and Uruguay to study and share experiences about what they considered subversive groups operating on the continent. Brazil did not attend, as the meeting fell during Carnival. Among the participants were PFA chief General Miguel Ángel Íñiguez, PFA inspectors Alberto Villar and Luis Margaride, and Víctor Castiglioni, general inspector of the Uruguayan Police Department and director of the National Directorate of Information and Intelligence (DNII). A three-person delegation travelled from Chile, composed of General Ernesto Baeza Michelsen, general director of the Investigations Police Force; his legal advisor, René Navarro Verdugo; and Air Force Colonel Mario Jahn Barrera, deputy director of the Directorate of National Intelligence (DINA).

As a result of this meeting, a new operational agreement was established to pursue thousands of people exiled in Argentina. Inspired by Interpol's model, this scheme included the creation of a secure communication channel, an intelligence center with data on subversive groups, and planned cross-border exchanges of police agents.

Zelmar Michelini, a Uruguayan senator of the leftist coalition Frente Amplio, had been living in exile in Buenos Aires for a year—since the day of the coup in Uruguay on June 27, 1973. He lived in room 75 of the Hotel Liberty, on Corrientes Avenue, with two of his sons, Zelmar and Luis Pedro.

From his exile in Argentina, Michelini, who worked as a journalist for several Argentine newspapers, including *La Opinión*, was closely monitored by the Uruguayan dictatorship. Argentine and Uruguayan police officers followed him constantly, positioning themselves in the hotel lobby or on the street corner outside. Michelini regularly warned his sons about Uruguayan Commissioner Hugo Campos Hermida's presence. Many other exiled Uruguayans had also spotted the commissioner and other Uruguayan police and military officers in the Argentine capital.

After returning to Buenos Aires from Italy, where in March 1974 he had delivered a powerful testimony before the Russell Tribunal II in Rome, denouncing the dramatic reality in Uruguay, including murder, the systematic use of torture and violence, and the destruction of the opposition and trade unions, Michelini began receiving death threats. In late June of that year, Uruguay's Ministry of the Interior revoked his passport. Other Uruguayan political refugees in Buenos Aires, such as Enrique Erro and Wilson Ferreira, were also kept under close surveillance.

LIBERTY HOTEL

On July 1, 1974, Argentine President Juan Domingo Perón died. Vice-president, María Estela Martínez de Perón, known as Isabelita—also his third wife—assumed the presidency. From that moment on, Argentina descended into a spiral of violence as its democracy crumbled.

The Minister of Social Welfare, José López Rega, nicknamed *El Brujo* (The Sorcerer), and a member of the *Propaganda Due* loggia, was the mastermind of the Argentine Anti-Communist Alliance, or the Triple A: a clandestine paramilitary gang responsible for the political assassination of hundreds of people between 1973 and 1976. Isabelita's government also issued the "annihilation decrees" in 1975, ordering the military to neutralize subversion in Argentina.

In the early morning on September 13, 1974, a squad of ten armed men, dressed in civilian clothes and wearing black gloves, broke into the home of Aurora Meloni and Daniel Banfi, Uruguayan exiles who lived with their daughters, Leticia and Valeria, in Haedo, in the province of Buenos Aires.

Aurora and Daniel immediately recognized the man in command: Commissioner Campos Hermida, whom they knew from a brief detention at the Police Headquarters in Montevideo after a student protest in 1969.

The men detained Daniel, Luis Latrónica—a Uruguayan exile recently arrived in Chile—and a family friend, Rivera Moreno. Within a few hours, two other Uruguayans, Nicasio Romero and Guillermo Jabif, were also kidnapped.

On October 29, the bodies of Daniel, Luís, and Guillermo appeared in a field in San Antonio de Areco, in Buenos Aires. They were riddled with bullets, tortured, and nearly unrecognizable. Rivera Moreno and Nicasio Romero had been released a few days earlier.

What happened to Banfi, Latrónica, and Jabif followed a pattern—still relatively unknown at the time—of clandestine detention, torture, and murder of exiled political activists. This pattern would become systematic during the Argentine dictatorship (1976–1983).

In mid-May, 1975, Jorge Fuentes Alarcón—a Chilean student leader and member of the Central Committee of the Movement of the Revolutionary Left (MIR)—and Amílcar Santucho—brother of Mario Roberto, the founder and leader of Argentina's PRT-ERP—were detained in Paraguay. They were travelling to Peru on a mission ordered by the Executive Committee of the Revolutionary Coordinating Junta (JCR), to which both belonged, with the goal of opening the junta to other South American organizations. Amílcar was the first person to be arrested at the border crossing in Puerto Itá Enramada on May 16; Jorge was seized the next day at the Hotel España in Asunción where he was staying.

In downtown Asunción, at 265 Presidente Franco Street, the main detention and torture center in Paraguay operated within the premises of the Investigations Department of the Capital Police. This is where Fuentes Alarcón and Santucho were taken after their detention, to be tortured. Because of their direct knowledge of the JCR's internal operation and infrastructure in Latin America and Europe, as well as those of the MIR and the PRT-ERP, Fuentes Alarcón and Santucho were repeatedly interrogated by agents of the Paraguayan, Chilean, and Argentine security forces.

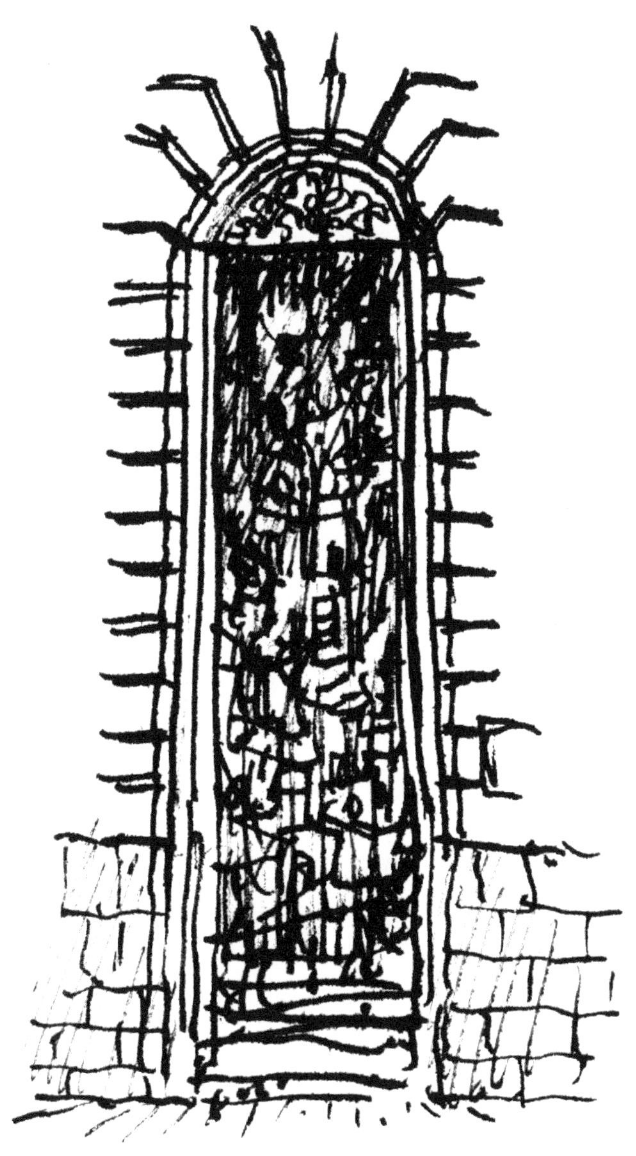

Paraguayan officers held Santucho until September 1979, when they deported him to Sweden. DINA agents apprehended Fuentes Alarcón and secretly transported him to Chile in September 1975. Back in his native country, several survivors of the clandestine detention centers known as Cuatro Álamos and Villa Grimaldi in Santiago saw Fuentes Alarcón. Having been a national student leader, many survivors easily recognized him, and several knew of his detention in Paraguay.

In Villa Grimaldi, agents subjected him to pitiful conditions: he suffered from scabies and other illnesses, and they constantly tortured and punished him. Despite this, his fellow prisoners remember how Jorge used to sing every time he went to the bathroom, as well as his solidarity toward other detainees and his attempts to lift their spirits in such a distressing environment. Fuentes Alarcón was last seen alive in January 1976.

The arrest of Fuentes Alarcón and Amílcar Santucho was the first major coordinated multilateral operation in South America. For this reason, in their 2016 verdict, the Argentine judges of the Federal Oral Tribunal n. 1 in Buenos Aires characterized the "Fuentes Alarcón–Santucho" case as a "pilot test" of Operation Condor.

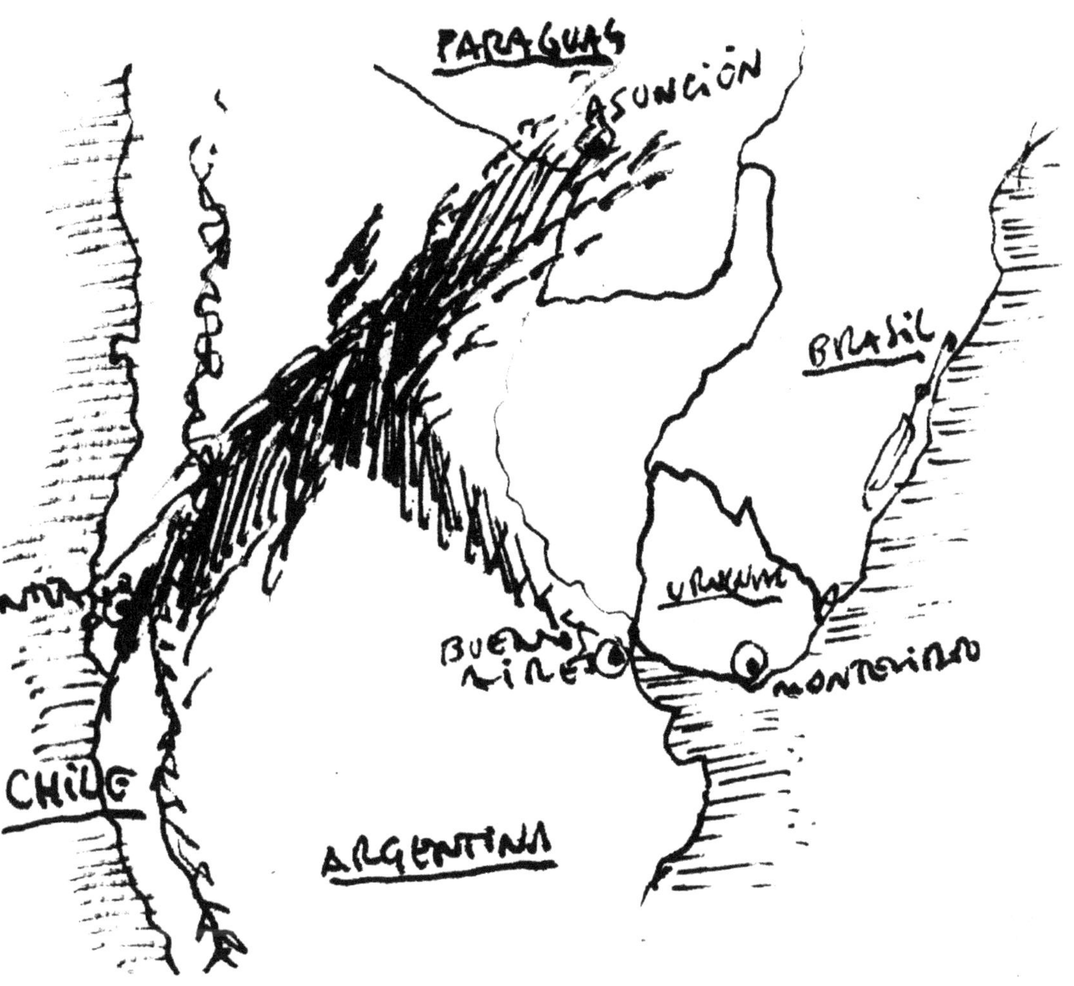

00143F 0010

149

00022F 0152

REPUBLICA DE CHILE
JUNTA MILITAR DE GOBIERNO
D.I.N.A.

Manuel Contreras Sepúlveda, Coronel
Director de Inteligencia Nacional, saluda muy atentamente al Sr. Jefe de Investigaciones del Paraguay, DON. PASTOR CORONEL y junto con tener el grato placer de saludarle le hace llegar los más sinceros agradecimientos por la cooperación prestada para facilitar las gestiones relativas a la Misión que debió cumplir mi personal en la hermana República del Paraguay, y estoy cierto que esta mutua cooperación continuará en forma siempre creciente para el logro de los objetivos comunes coincidentes de ambos Servicios.

CONTRERAS, hace propicia la oportunidad para testimoniarle los sentimientos de su consideración más distinguida, y rogándole considerarlo a sus muy gratas órdenes en ésta.

SANTIAGO, 25 DE SEPTIEMBRE 75.=

On July 26, 1975, Uruguayan leftist militants, particularly members of the Anarchist Federation of Uruguay, founded the Party for the Victory of the People (Partido por la Victoria del Pueblo—PVP). Over 1000 militants took part in the so-called "final gathering," held in a house in Lanús, in the province of Buenos Aires.

The PVP's objectives were to galvanize opposition to the Uruguayan dictatorship from abroad and to foster the return to democracy. Its leaders at the time were trade unionists Gerardo Gatti and León Duarte.

3. *The* FOUNDATION *of* OPERATION CONDOR

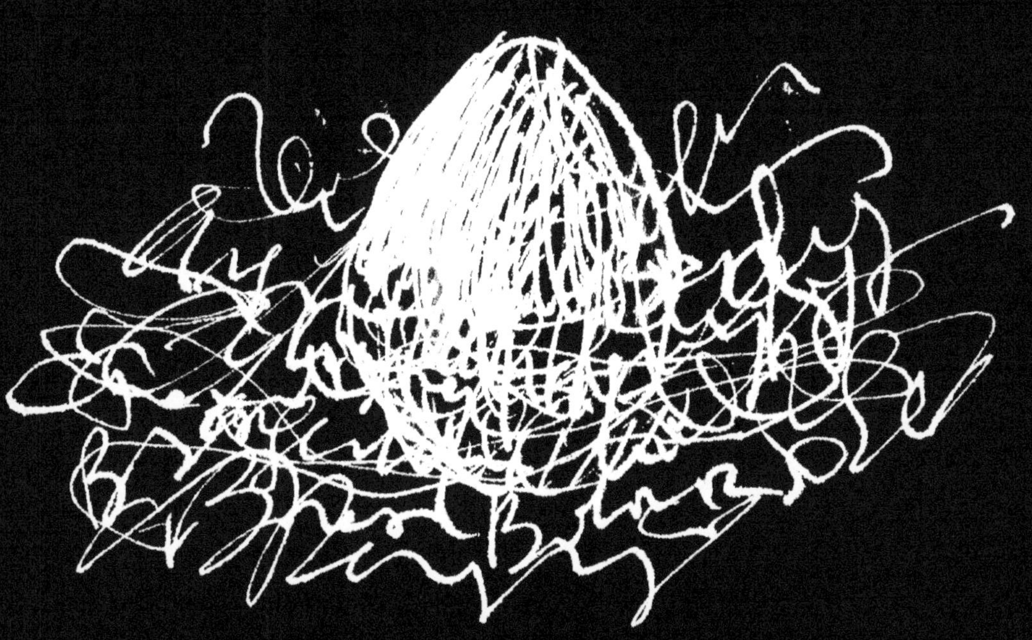

00143F 0011

00022F 0153

Manuel Contreras Sepúlveda, Coronel
Director de Inteligencia Nacional, saluda atentamente al Sr. General de División DON. FRANCISCO BRITES, Jefe de la Policía de la República del Paraguay, y tiene el alto honor de invitarle a una Reunión de Trabajo de Inteligencia Nacional que se realizará en Santiago de Chile, entre los días 25 de Noviembre y 01 de Diciembre de 1975.

La Reunión tiene carácter de Estrictamente Secreta, y se adjunta Temario propuesto y programa tentativo.

El Coronel CONTRERAS, ruega al Sr. General BRITES, honrarle con su presencia, y si lo estima hacerse acompañar por algunos asesores, ya que espera que esta Reunión pueda ser la base de una excelente coordinación y un mejor accionar en beneficio de la Seguridad Nacional de nuestros respectivos Países.

SANTIAGO, OCTUBRE DE 1975.

In August 1975, the director of Chile's Directorate of National Intelligence (DINA), Colonel Manuel Contreras, embarked on an ambitious mission to establish a system for regional coordination against subversive activities. The first stop in Contreras's journey was Washington D.C., where he met with General Vernon Walters, deputy director of the CIA. He then travelled to Venezuela.

In October, Contreras sent the second in command of the DINA, Colonel Mario Jahn Barrera, to Paraguay, Argentina, Bolivia, Brazil, and Uruguay. His task was to deliver invitations personally to a Working Meeting on National Intelligence,

to be held in Santiago from November 25 to December 1, 1975. The DINA would cover all expenses for up to three delegates per country.

The region's intelligence chiefs met at the Academy of War on Alameda Avenue in Santiago. Its stated objective was to coordinate the actions of South American countries in the name of national security. The meeting's program argued that subversion no longer respected national borders and was coordinating its actions on a continental level. Bilateral agreements or simple gentlemen's agreements, they claimed, were no longer sufficient—a continental response was now required.

1. This Organization will be called CONDOR, by the unanimous approval of a motion presented by the Uruguayan

Delegation in honor of the host country.

On November 28, 1975, in Santiago, the heads of the Argentine, Bolivian, Chilean, Paraguayan, and Uruguayan delegations agreed to establish the Condor System to organize future actions against subversion at the regional level. Those who signed the Minutes of the Conclusions of the First Interamerican Meeting on National Intelligence were:

- Army Colonel José A. Fons, deputy director of the Defense Information System (SID), Uruguay's military intelligence
- Colonel Benito Guanes Serrano, head of Paraguay's Military Intelligence
- Army Major Carlos Mena Burgos, deputy chief of the Intelligence Service of the Bolivian state
- Navy Captain Jorge Casas, assistant secretary of Argentina's Secretariat of State Information (SIDE)
- And the host, Colonel Manuel Contreras

The attendees unanimously named the new organization CONDOR, in honor of Chile and its national symbol, the condor, after the Uruguayan delegation presented a motion they agreed with. Four characteristics defined the system:

- Bilateral or multilateral contacts for the exchange of information related to subversion
- The creation of a coordinating office to provide information on people and organizations considered subversive
- A system for periodic contact among intelligence services
- A three-stage coordination system

On January 30, 1976, the founding agreement was to take effect after being ratified by all participating countries. New member countries could only join the system with the approval of all founding members.

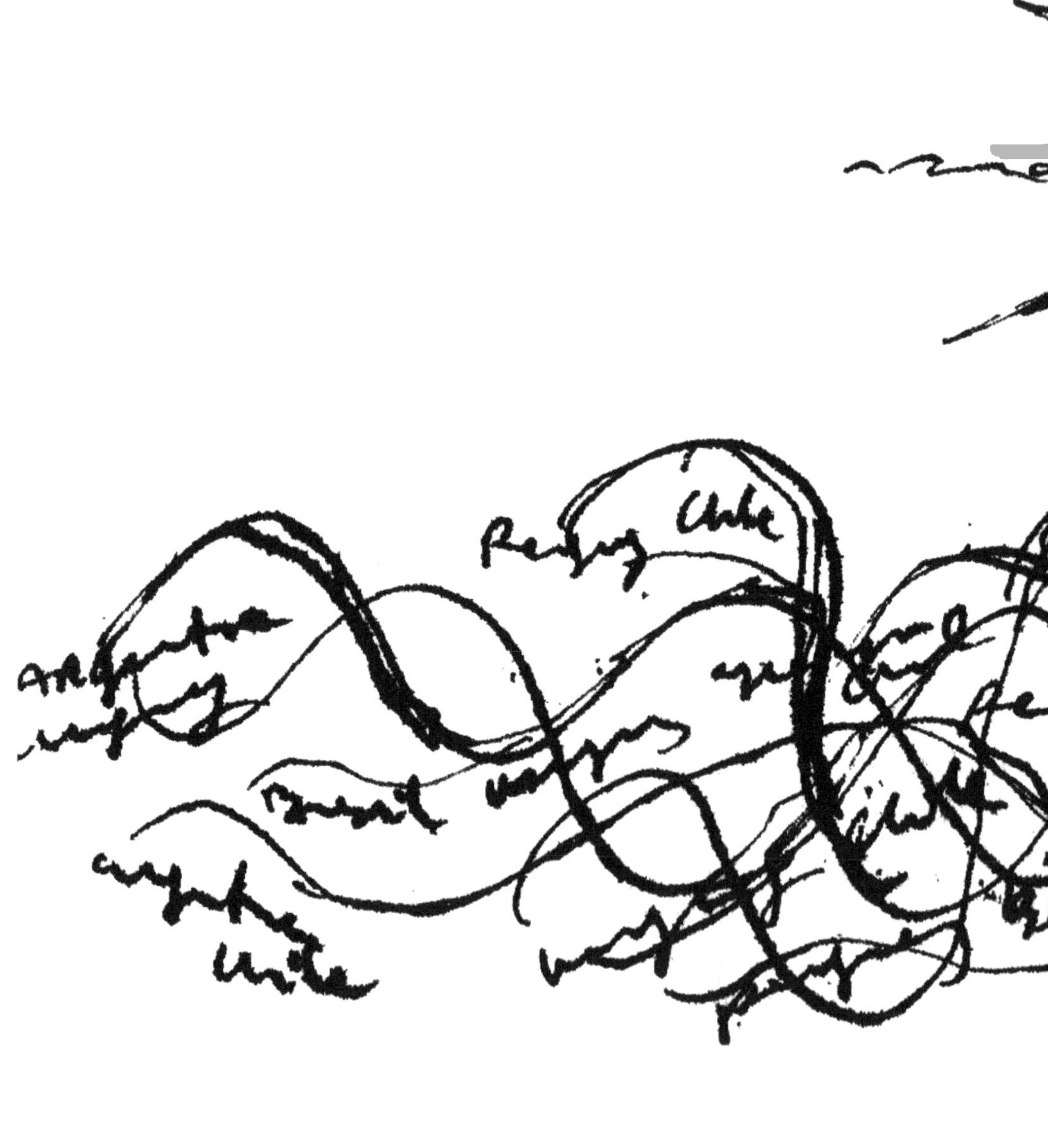

4. *The* SAFE HEAVEN BECOMES *a* DEATH TRAP

On March 24, 1976, a military junta led by Army General Jorge Rafael Videla together with Navy Admiral Emilio Eduardo Massera and Air Force Brigadier General Orlando Ramón Agosti, seized power in Argentina.

The so-called National Reorganization Process that followed sought to annihilate all forms of political, social, trade union, or student opposition—anyone considered an "internal enemies." The coup eliminated all democratic institutions in Argentina and marked a turning point in cross-border repression. Thousands of South American refugees who had made Argentina their home since the 1960s now found themselves fatally trapped. Surrounded by countries under dictatorial rule, they had nowhere left to flee.

As had already happened in neighboring dictatorships, repression in Argentina was carried out in secret. Its aim was to subject the entire society to terror, paralyzing any opposition to the political and economic models the regime sought to impose by force. A campaign of forced disappearances was launched across the country.

This systematic plan of repression relied on tight territorial control and a vast network of more than 800 clandestine detention centers (CDCs). These secret facilities, some in operation since 1974, became widely used after the coup to enable the clandestine detention, torture, interrogation, and disappearance of people.

The CDCs were located in a variety of buildings—police stations, military barracks, commercial premises, and even private homes. The CDC most closely associated with Operation Condor was Automotores Orletti, which operated from May 11 to November 3, 1976, in a two-story auto repair shop at 3519/21 Venancio Flores Street, in the Floresta neighborhood of Buenos Aires, facing the Sarmiento railway line. Approximately three hundred people were detained there, most of them foreigners—especially Uruguayans, Chileans, and Cubans—and many were disappeared.

Task forces, known as *patotas*, made up of police, military, and civilian personnel, carried out the systematic repression. Often using green Ford Falcon vehicles, these groups kidnapped their victims in broad daylight, on the streets, at their workplaces, or in the early morning from their homes or those of friends and family. The operations were violent: besides taking the victims, they seized their belongings and looted their properties.

The campaign of repression included kidnapping, torture, sexual violence, executions, forced disappearance, home invasions, theft, appropriation of babies—around 500 in Argentina alone—as well as extortion and threats, carried out across the territories of Operation Condor member countries.

Both military and civilian resources at the disposal of member states fueled Operation Condor's transnational terror. Military and police forces took part, along with diplomatic personnel through embassy and consulate networks—privileged sites for spying on militants in exile—and civilian border agents.

What had been considered a haven...

...ended up being a trap.

On May 20, 1976, in Buenos Aires, the Uruguayan dictatorship murdered four of its citizens living in exile in the Argentine capital: Members of Parliament Héctor Gutiérrez Ruiz and Zelmar Michelini, and militants Rosario Barredo and William Whitelaw.

In the early morning of May 13, Whitelaw, Barredo, their two children—María Victoria and Máximo Fernando—and Rosario's eldest daughter, Gabriela, had been arrested at their home in the Caballito neighborhood. They were held at the CDC on Bacacay Street, on the same block as Orletti. Later, their paternal grandfather traveled from Uruguay and took custody of the children after their release from captivity. Michelini and Gutiérrez Ruiz were kidnapped in the early morning on May 18, just hours apart. They were likely imprisoned at the Bacacay or Orletti CDCs.

On September 21, 1976, in Washington D.C., Operation Condor's networks enabled the Chilean dictatorship to carry out a terrorist assassination on U.S. soil. DINA agent Michael Townley, together with anti-Castro Cuban militants, placed a bomb under the car of Orlando Letelier, a former ambassador and minister in Salvador Allende's government. The explosion killed Letelier and his colleague from the Institute of Political Studies, Ronni Moffitt, as they were driving to work. Ronni's husband, Michael, survived.

The investigation into the Letelier-Moffitt murder, and the subsequent pressure from the United States, led to the closure of Chile's DINA in August 1977. A much weaker organization, the National Information Center (Central Nacional de Informaciones) replaced it. But only months earlier, the DINA had carried out what was likely its last major operation abroad.

In Argentina and Chile, DINA and Argentine security agents arrested nineteen members of the communist parties of both countries (PCCh and PCA, respectively). These militants had been involved in an operation to send financial resources to Chile, via Buenos Aires, where the PCCh were attempting to regroup after the persecution unleashed against its leaders by Chilean security forces in 1976.

Between March and April, 1977 PCCh leaders Ricardo Ignacio Ramírez Herrera and Héctor Heraldo Velásquez Mardones left their exile in Hungary to establish a party base in Buenos Aires and facilitate the transfer of funds. In the Argentine capital, they contacted members of the PCA, who often helped recent Chilean exiles find work and housing. Meanwhile, another leader, Américo Zorrilla, entrusted the Swiss/Chilean citizen Alexei Vladimir Jaccard Siegler with the mission of traveling from Geneva to Buenos Aires to deliver a large amount of money. Jaccard was the ideal candidate: as an experienced PCCh militant, he had been exiled in Switzerland, held Swiss nationality, and had not visited Chile since 1974.

Jaccard left Milan on May 14, 1977, bound for Buenos Aires, carrying a Swiss passport. His task was to deliver the funds to Ramírez and Velásquez before continuing onwards to Santiago. The day after his arrival, apparently violating security protocols, he briefly visited his mother, sister, and brother-in-law in the locality of San Miguel, where his relatives were living as refugees while awaiting exile in France.

On May 16, Jaccard, Ramírez, and Velásquez disappeared. The next day, police officers collected Jaccard's belongings from the Hotel Bristol, where he had stayed. In the following days, Argentine police and military personnel detained twelve other members of the PCA, some of whom had closely assisted the Chileans. Only three of them survived.

The operation continued on both sides of the Andes for several more weeks. On May 29, Argentine security forces detained the Chilean banker Jacobo Stoulman and his wife Matilde Pessa Mois upon their arrival at the Ezeiza International Airport in Buenos Aires. Stoulman, who owned currency exchange offices in Chile and Argentina, had been tasked with traveling to Buenos Aires to collect the funds for the PCCh. On May 27, in Santiago, DINA agents captured Ruiter Enrique Correa Arce, who was responsible for receiving money for the PCCh. Agents found his severely tortured body near the Mapocho River the next morning. On June 7, Hernán Soto Gálvez, another participant in the operation in Chile, was forced into an unmarked black car without a license plate by three agents. He was never seen again.

Military officers then launched a cover-up campaign to counter the international pressure, especially from Swiss authorities, which were inquiring about Jaccard's whereabouts. Documents were falsified, and others were created to suggest that Jaccard had arrived in Santiago on May 26 and left for Montevideo on June 12. Meanwhile, lawyer Ambrosio Rodríguez, a man close to the Chilean dictatorship, was hired by the Stoulman family to investigate the couple's fate. Although officers of the First Army Corps in Buenos Aires confirmed they handed Jacobo and Matilde over to DINA agents, Rodríguez provided a different version. He claimed the couple was involved in funding guerrilla uprisings in Argentina, paralyzing all efforts to uncover the truth.

5. UNVEILING OPERATION CONDOR: *The* FIRST ALLEGATIONS

Unlike its neighbors, Argentina had a tradition of human rights activism that predated the dictatorship. The Argentine Human Rights League (Liga Argentina por los Derechos del Hombre), founded in December 1937, was the country's first human rights organization.

In December 1975, as the nation spiraled into violence and freedom came under threat from the Triple A and the Armed Forces, a group of politicians, religious leaders, and trade unionists created the Permanent Assembly for Human Rights (Asamblea Permanente por los Derechos Humanos—APDH). Its mission was to defend democracy and uphold human rights.

After the coup on March 24, 1976, new organizations emerged, formed by relatives of the disappeared and detained. Among them, Relatives of the Disappeared and Detained for Political Reasons (Familiares de Desaparecidos y Detenidos por Razones Políticas), founded in 1976, and the Mothers and Grandmothers of Plaza de Mayo (Madres y Abuelas de Plaza de Mayo) founded in 1977. These groups, along with others such as the Peace and Justice Service (Servicio Paz y Justicia—SERPAJ) and the Ecumenical Movement for Human Rights (Movimiento Ecuménico por los Derechos Humanos—MEDH), denounced cases of forced disappearance. The Mothers and Grandmothers of Plaza de Mayo, in particular, demanded the return of their sons and daughters alive. They also demanded that babies born while their mothers were secretly detained be reunited with their biological families.

25 • MAY

Denunciations of serious human rights violations reached as far as the United States and Europe, as well as international organizations such as the United Nations, the Inter-American Commission on Human Rights, and Amnesty International.

In 1976, in Washington D.C., U.S. Congressman Edward Koch, a Democrat, introduced a proposal to suspend military aid to the Uruguayan dictatorship because of its human rights record. The measure, known as the "Koch Amendment," was adopted in late 1976 and effectively halted the payment of three million dollars Uruguay was scheduled to receive in 1977.

On November 3, 1976, two PRT-ERP militants, José Ramón Morales and Graciela Vidaillac, escaped from the clandestine center in Buenos Aires where they were being held, after a gunfight with their captors.

As they fled in panic, they caught sight of a worn sign: at the top, it read "Automotores S.A.," and below the words "Cortell, Cortell, Cortell." In their haste, they misread it as "Automotores Orletti."

There, prisoners were held in inhuman conditions on the ground floor. On the upper floor, Argentine and foreign agents used two rooms as offices; the others served as cells. In the back, agents used a large room for torture and interrogation.

Survivors recall the constant sound of trains, the code words operación sésamo (Operation Sesame) used to open the metal shutter, and the sound of children playing at a nearby school.

On March 23, 1977, during a press conference in London marking the first anniversary of Argentina's military coup, Amnesty International revealed the testimony of the Uruguayan jounalist Enrique Rodríguez Larreta Piera, who survived illegal imprisonment, tortue, and clandestine transfer from Argentina to Uruguay.

Even at great personal risk, since his family still lived in Uruguay, the 55-year-old journalist recounted that in July 1976 he had traveled from Montevideo to Buenos Aires after learning of his son's disappearance. Together with his daughter-in-law, he tirelessly denounced the situation until, a few days later, they too were kidnapped.

Both were held and tortured at Automotores Orletti alongside thirty fellow Uruguayans, including trade unionists Gerardo Gatti and León Duarte. On July 24, the journalist, his son, his daughter-in-law, and twenty-one other Uruguayans were transferred to Uruguay on a secret flight. There, he spent five more months in two clandestine prisons before being freed shortly before Christmas.

His testimony became a crucial piece of evidence demonstrating the existence of repressive coordination between Argentina and Uruguay as early as 1977.

6. CROSS BORDER REPRESSION: FIVE *in* ASUNCION

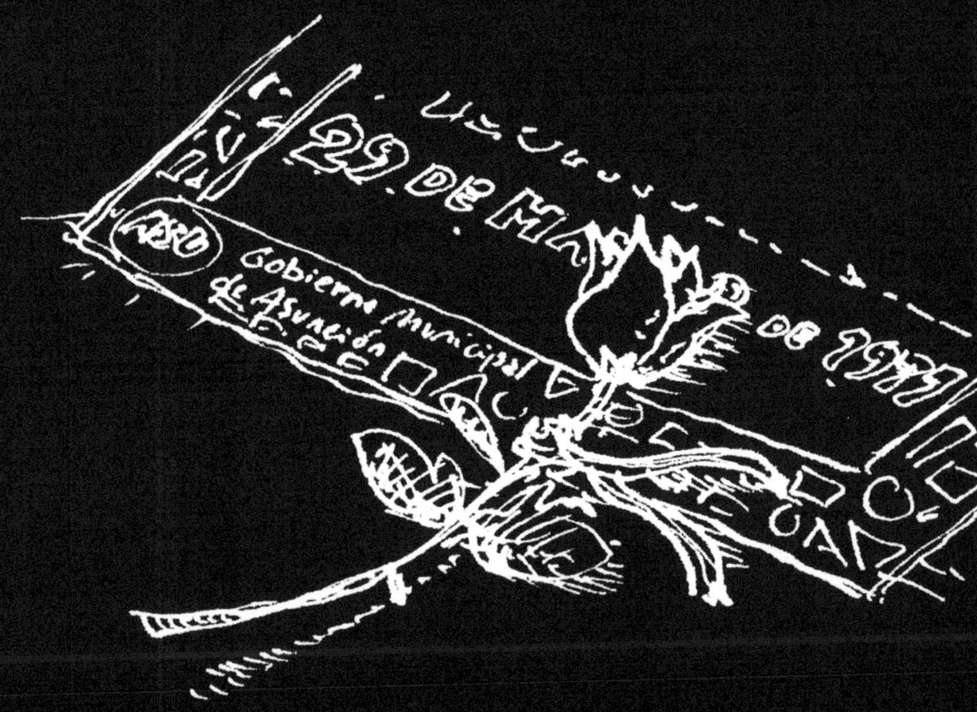

Argentine nationals, José Luis Nell, Alejandro Logoluso, and Dora Landi, along with Uruguayan citizens Nelson Santana and Gustavo Inzaurralde, were abducted in Asunción, Paraguay on March 29, 1977. Nearly five decades later, they remain disappeared. All were militants of different political parties and movements brutally repressed by South America's dictatorships during the years of state terrorism. They had arrived in Paraguay a few weeks before their kidnapping, hoping to obtain false passports that would allow them and other activists to seek safety in Europe.

The ordeal these five militants endured reveals the modus operandi of Operation Condor. They were first persecuted in their home countries—some spent time in prison, their homes were repeatedly raided—and all were forced to flee for safety elsewhere.

Gustavo Inzaurralde was active in the Anarchist Federation of Uruguay and in the Uruguayan Teachers' Federation. He was detained in 1969. In prison, Gustavo met Argentine José Luis Nell, who had moved to Montevideo because his son—also named José Luis and a Tupamaro member—was imprisoned in Punta Carretas Prison. The elder Nell, a member of Argentina's Peronist Party, befriended Inzaurralde during visits to his son.

After his release in 1971, Inzaurralde went first to Chile and then, following Pinochet's coup in 1973, settled with his partner, María del Carmen Posse Merino, in Lanús, in the province of Buenos Aires. By early 1977, Inzaurralde was the last remaining leader of the Party for the Victory of the People (PVP) in the Southern Cone.

Nelson Santana was active in the Workers and Students' Resistance group in Uruguay. Due to relentless persecution, he also moved to Buenos Aires in 1975. There, he joined the PVP and, like Inzaurralde, survived the wave of killings unleashed against the party's militants in Argentina between June and October 1976.

The Argentines Alejandro Logoluso and Marta Landi met at the university in La Plata. Both were members of the Peronist Youth and were persecuted for it. The security forces repeatedly raided Alejandro's home in Mar del Plata.

The story of these five individuals shows how, through the inner workings of Operation Condor, victims were monitored even in exile and later arrested in Paraguay. There, an international task force interrogated and tortured them—evidence of regional collaboration between armed forces and the fluid exchange of information. A document from Paraguay's Archives of Terror confirms the clandestine transfer of the five from Asunción to Buenos Aires on May 16, 1977.

José Luis Nell Granada, at 67, had already lost his wife, María Eloísa Tacchi, who was injured in the bombing of Plaza de Mayo in Buenos Aires in 1955 and later died of cancer. His son, guerrilla fighter José Luis Nell Tacchi, took his own life in 1974, after being disabled by a bullet during the shootout at Ezeiza on June 20, 1973—the day Perón returned to Argentina after nearly eighteen years of exile. In June 1976, his daughter-in-law, Lucía Cullen, a social activist in Barrio 31 who worked alongside Father Carlos Mugica, was disappeared.

At that point, Nell later said, he felt he had nothing left to lose and decided to help victims of political persecution in Argentina.

During the dictatorship, Nell actively assisted Argentine and foreign militants who needed documentation to leave the country and seek political asylum elsewhere. His house at 123 Domingo Portela Street, in the Flores neighborhood of Buenos Aires, was a safe house where many refugees stayed. Because he was not an active militant at that time, Nell could move freely and complete bureaucratic formalities with ease.

In Argentina, he reunited with his friend Inzaurralde. Together, they organized an operation to escape to Paraguay, purchase false passports, and travel to Brazil, where a United Nations refugee office operated—before continuing on to Europe. In late January 1977, Nell made an initial trip to Asunción and settled in a boarding house at 884 Fulgencio Moreno Street, in the center of the Paraguayan capital.

On January 27, 1977, Dora Landi and Alejandro Logoluso also left Argentina due to the political persecution. Alejandro's house had already been raided three times. Their plan was to reach Brazil and from there apply for asylum in Europe. They first traveled to Misiones province, northeastern Argentina, then continued to Asunción to obtain the documents needed for the next leg of their journey. Alejandro traveled under the false name of Guillermo Oscar Stagni. That same day, intruders raided his house in Mar del Plata again. They threatened his sister Laura and asked for him.

DESPACHO
EQUIPAJES

Upon arriving in Asunción, Alejandro Logoluso and Dora Landi found an advertisement in the Paraguayan newspaper ABC for a boarding house on Fulgencio Moreno Street—the same one where José Luis Nell was staying. It was there they met, by chance.

On April 20, Argentine dictator Jorge Videla was scheduled to make an official visit to Paraguay to meet with his counterpart, dictator Alfredo Stroessner. In the weeks leading up to the trip, police surveillance intensified in Asunción. Since the beginning of 1977, Paraguay had seen a sharp escalation in repression, which extended to Paraguayan exiles abroad.

Between October 1976 and February 1977, ten exiles were abducted in Argentina and forcibly returned to Paraguay, including disappeared doctor Agustín Goiburú and several militants of the Paraguayan Communist Party, such as Lidia Cabrera.

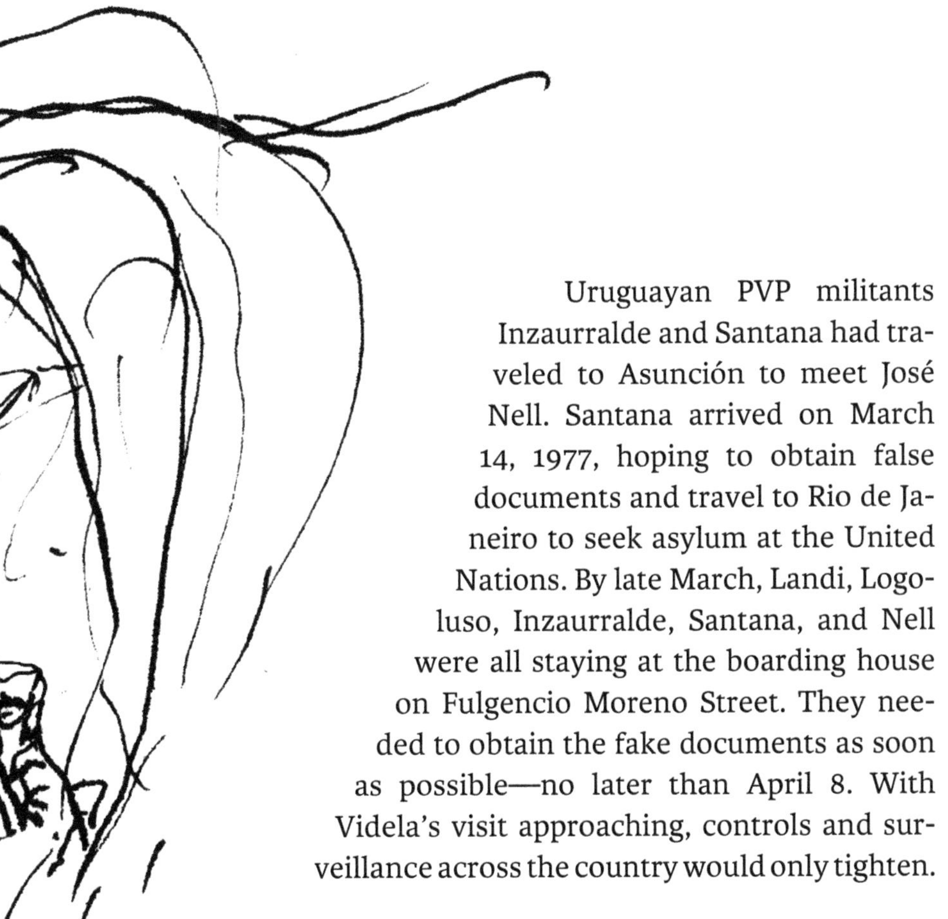

Uruguayan PVP militants Inzaurralde and Santana had traveled to Asunción to meet José Nell. Santana arrived on March 14, 1977, hoping to obtain false documents and travel to Rio de Janeiro to seek asylum at the United Nations. By late March, Landi, Logoluso, Inzaurralde, Santana, and Nell were all staying at the boarding house on Fulgencio Moreno Street. They needed to obtain the fake documents as soon as possible—no later than April 8. With Videla's visit approaching, controls and surveillance across the country would only tighten.

On March 28, a woman went to the Investigations Department of the Capital Police in Asunción to report that, while at the Identification Directorate, she had overheard another woman, named Nilda León Samaniego, say she was processing documents for around 80 or 100 Argentines. They had all fled their country and were going to pay 30,000 guaraníes per document. The informant approached Nilda, offered to help with the paperwork, and arranged to meet at her house the next day.

Based on this information, the police set up surveillance at the informant's home. On March 29, Gustavo Inzaurralde, Nelson Santana, and Nilda León Samaniego were arrested there.

Later that day, as part of the same operation targeting counterfeit documents, agents of the Capital Police raided the boarding house at 884 Fulgencio Moreno Street. There they arrested all the boarders—including Alejandro Logoluso, Dora Landi, and José Nell—along with the owner of the lodging.

José Nell, Gustavo Inzaurralde, Nelson Santana, Dora Landi, and Alejandro Logoluso were taken to the Investigations Department of the Capital Police, where they were interrogated and tortured.

Operation Condor, established in Santiago de Chile at the end of 1975 and by 1977 encompassing Argentina, Bolivia, Brazil, Chile, Paraguay, and Uruguay, was a sophisticated, ambitious, and institutionalized system of transnational repression.

It had three main pillars. First, a database in Santiago that centralized intelligence information on individuals and subversive groups under surveillance across the continent. Second, an operational axis known as "Condoreje," which included a command and action office in Buenos Aires, staffed by agents from the member countries. Third, an encrypted and secret communication system called "Condortel."

Through Condortel, which also relied on a US communications facility in the Panama Canal Zone, Condor member countries could quickly exchange intelligence information on targets and joint operations. In their communications, Condortel used a simple alphabetical code for the five original Condor countries: Condor 1 was Argentina, 2 Bolivia, 3 Chile, 4 Paraguay, 5 Uruguay, while Brazil had observer status. In early 1978, with the addition of two new members, Peru became Condor 6 and Ecuador Condor 7.

The ultrasecret *Teseo* (Theseus) unit is also worth mentioning. Composed of agents from Argentina, Chile, and Uruguay, they received special training in Buenos Aires in late 1976. Its members were then sent to Europe to murder militants living there, especially in France. Bolivia, Brazil, and Paraguay chose not to participate in Teseo's operations. Most of these assassination attempts outside South America were ultimately either unsuccessful or called off.

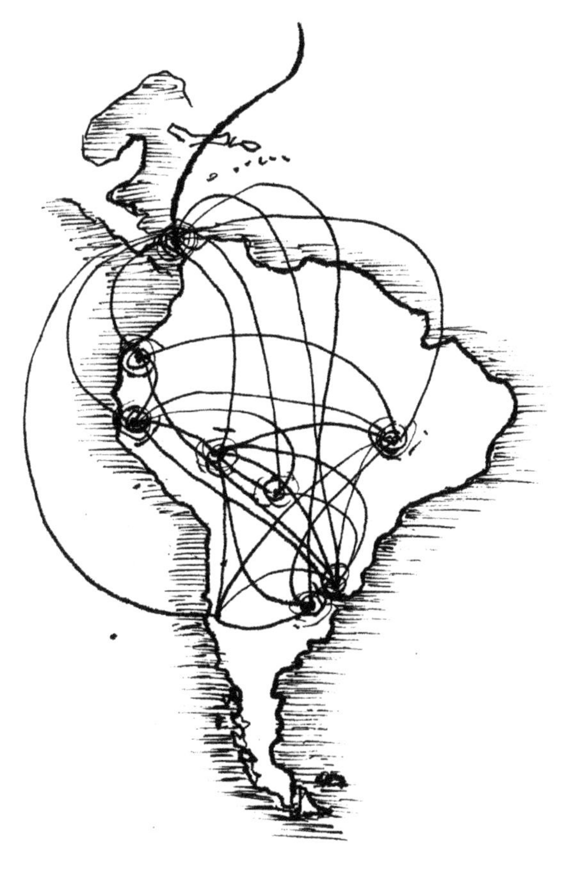

HAGELIN-CRYPTOS

At the Investigations Department, Nell, Inzaurralde, Santana, Landi, and Logoluso were interrogated and tortured—also by Argentine and Uruguayan agents who traveled to Asunción for that purpose.

A document from the Paraguayan Archives of Terror narrates how joint interrogations took place on April 5 and 6, 1977, with the participation of seven intelligence officers from Argentina, Paraguay, and Uruguay. Among them were Colonel Benito Guanes Serrano of Paraguayan military intelligence and Colonel Carlos Calcagno of the Uruguayan SID.

The foreign officers brought relevant documents to assist in the interrogations. These included PVP organizational charts, prepared by the Uruguayan Army, illustrating the party's structure, and a list of 63 wanted members of the Popular Revolutionary Organization–33 Orientals (OPR-33).

Parallel to the interrogations in Asunción, on April 6, an operation also unfolded at Nell's house in Buenos Aires, where Chilean refugee Jorge Sagaute Herrera was staying.

Sagaute Herrera had been the Director of Aeronautics of the Chilean Air Force and had moved to Argentina in the mid-1970s to accompany his sons and daughters, who were being persecuted by Pinochet's dictatorship. A friend of Nell's, he was tortured and killed in Nell's home in the Flores neighborhood. In 2019, the Argentine Forensic Anthropology Team identified his body in the Lomas de Zamora cemetery.

Two weeks after the operation at Nell's house, Argentine dictator Videla's official visit to Paraguay took place—the very event that had prompted heightened surveillance and controls.

On April 20, Videla—accompanied by his wife and a large entourage including the Chancellor, Vice Admiral César Guzzetti, and the Minister of Economy, José Martínez de Hoz—arrived in Asunción. It was the first official meeting between the two presidents. During the visit, Videla and Stroessner participated in a military parade on Mariscal López Avenue, riding in a white Chevrolet convertible.

The two dictators also attended public events and signed declarations on cooperation for the hydroelectric projects of Yacyretá and Corpus on the Paraná River. They reaffirmed their collaboration in the fight against subversion and terrorism.

When the visit took place, Landi, Logoluso, Nell, Inzaurralde, and Santana remained confined at the Investigations Department in Asunción. Paraguayan survivors detained at the same time reported that the five foreigners were repeatedly tortured.

The Paraguayan police held the five Argentines and Uruguayans in the dungeons until mid-May 1977. During that time, several Paraguayan detainees who had been brought there after being abducted in Argentina saw them, including Sotero Franco, Esteban Cabrera, Lidia Cabrera, and Domingo Rolón Centurión.

Dora Landi shared a cell with Lidia Cabrera. She told Lidia about her repeated abuse and torture; on one occasion, agents gave her a pill to force her to talk, leaving her completely disoriented. Dora was terrified that the Paraguayan police would hand her and Alejandro over to the Argentines. She believed that if they were sent back to Argentina, they would not survive.

A few days later, the Uruguayan dictatorship decided Inzaurralde and Santana's fate, possibly after a meeting by the Joint Chiefs of Staff on April 30. Composed at that time by Vice Admiral Hugo León Márquez, Lieutenant General Julio César Vadora, and Brigadier General Dante Paladini, the Joint Chiefs of Staff were the core of the dictatorship's government and military power. At that meeting, the commanders evaluated the statements Inzaurralde had made during his detention in Paraguay.

On May 16, agents of the Capital Police handed Nell, Inzaurralde, Santana, Landi, and Logoluso over to two Argentine intelligence officers. The five were transferred onto a Hawker Siddeley 125-400B twin-jet airplane, registration 5T-30–0653, the personal-use aircraft of Admiral Eduardo Massera, Commander in Chief of the Argentine Navy.

Piloted by Captain José Abdala (the false name employed by Captain Luis D'Imperio of the Naval Intelligence Service), the plane took off for Buenos Aires.

The clandestine detention and torture center known as El Club Atlético was located in the San Telmo neighborhood of Buenos Aires. This secret jail operated from February to December 1977 in the basement of a building belonging to the Provision and Workshop Service of the Administrative Division of Argentina's Federal Police. Up to 1,500 people were held there during its operation.

On May 26, 1977, Ricardo Peidró, a survivor of El Club Atlético, shared a cell with Gustavo Inzaurralde for one day. Inzaurralde told him about his militancy in the PVP and his detention in Paraguay as he tried to travel to Sweden to reunite with his pregnant partner. He also said that he had been brought to Argentina to be interrogated by Uruguayan officers. That was the last anyone ever knew of him. Inzaurralde was the only one of the five seen at a clandestine center after their secret deportation to Argentina.

In mid-July 1977, in Uruguay, the Joint Chiefs of Staff and the SID began publishing wanted notices for Inzaurralde and Santana. This was a common procedure during the dictatorship, used to cover up disappearances and kidnappings. Other notices followed until the statute of limitations on the crimes for which they were being sought eventually rendered them void.

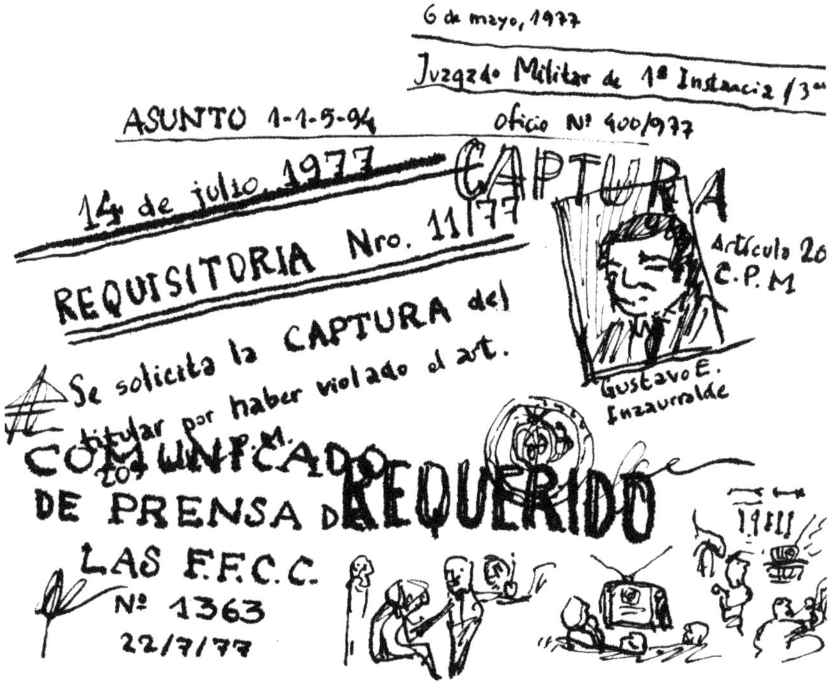

6 de mayo, 1977

Juzgado Militar de 1ª Instancia / 3ª

ASUNTO 1-1-5-94

Oficio Nº 400/977

14 de julio 1977

CAPTURA

REQUISITORIA Nro. 11/77

Se solicita la CAPTURA del titular por haber violado el art. 20 C.P.M.

Artículo 20 C.P.M

Gustavo E. Inzaurralde

COMUNICADO DE PRENSA DE LAS F.F.C.C. Nº 1363 22/7/77

REQUERIDO

While searching for Alejandro Logoluso and Dora Landi in 1977 and 1978, their relatives received false leads, and Paraguayan police officers even harassed and defrauded them in Paraguay.

In the Operation Condor trial in Argentina, Nidia Landi, Dora's sister, testified that the family received various conflicting reports about Dora's whereabouts, raising false hopes. Even the Argentine consul in Paraguay gave them fabricated information, stating that Dora had been handed over to Argentina in late November 1977.

In May 1977, relatives had traveled to a hotel in Foz do Iguaçu, in Brazil, to deliver money demanded in exchange for Dora and Alejandro's lives. Despite making payment, the couple never reappeared alive.

7. TEARING DOWN OPERATION CONDOR

Throughout 1977, reports of serious human rights violations in the Southern Cone, particularly in Argentina, grew increasingly frequent. In October of that year, the French newspaper *Le Monde* issued the first call to boycott the 1978 soccer World Cup in Argentina. France soon became the epicenter of international allegations regarding human rights violations in that South American country. Solidarity campaigns across the democratic world supported people living under dictatorships in South America.

Uruguay
BOYCOTT COUP DU MONDE
URUGUAY
4 YEARS OF TORTURE
URUGUAY
BOICOT

In 1978, the long-standing and traditionally bitter rivalry between Argentina and Chile resurfaced after a temporary respite during the years of Operation Condor. An old territorial dispute over the precise demarcation of the border along the Beagle Channel in the southern Tierra del Fuego—particularly concerning sovereignty over the three islands of Picton, Lennox, and Nueva—brought the two countries to the brink of war once again, after all attempts of at negotiation failed.

By November, both countries' armed forces had reached maximum alert, and a military clash seemed likely in the far south of the continent. The Argentine military adopted increasingly incendiary rhetoric. General Carlos Suárez Mason, commander of the Argentine First Army Corps, declared that if the Beagle issue did not reach a resolution in a meeting between the two countries' Foreign Affairs ministers scheduled for December, Argentina would occupy the three disputed islands and fight Chile "to the bitter end."

Just hours before the conflict was set to begin on December 22, 1978, the recently appointed Pope John Paul II's peace appeal averted hostilities. Five days later, the Pope sent his personal representative, Cardinal Antonio Samorè, to Buenos Aires, where he played a key role in de-escalating the situation. Negotiations included a meeting in Montevideo between the Argentine and Chilean Foreign Ministers, where they signed an agreement requesting Vatican mediation. It was not until November 1984 that the two countries signed the Treaty of Peace and Friendship, which definitively established the limits of their southern borders.

It was in this tense context of the Beagle Channel dispute that, on November 24, 1978, Chilean DINA agent Enrique Arancibia Clavel was arrested in Buenos Aires for espionage. He had been reporting on Argentina's military maneuvers in the south.

Arancibia Clavel had begun operating in Buenos Aires in late 1974. Coming from a traditionally military family and connected to extreme right groups, he was reportedly recruited as a DINA agent by the agency's director himself, Colonel Manuel Contreras, because of his extensive network of contacts in Argentina.

In 1979, eight families of disappeared militants founded the Center for Legal and Social Studies (Centro de Estudios Legales y Sociales—CELS) in Buenos Aires. Among them were lawyer Emilio Mignone and his wife Angélica, lawyer Augusto Conte, and professors Noemí Labrune and Carmen Aguiar de Lapacó.

Like the Argentine Human Rights League and APDH, CELS's key strategies for combating impunity included denouncing and documenting human rights violations, as well as pursuing legal action. The organization also sought to shed light on the state's role in political repression and to explain how state terrorism operated by analyzing patterns and data. It worked to build international networks and pressure thejudiciary.

By the early 1980s, Argentina's dictatorship faced mounting problems: trade union demonstrations, economic recession, and persistent reports of human rights violations.

In 1982, the military junta, led by Lieutenant General Leopoldo Galtieri, recovered the Falkland Islands. The decision was primarily political—an attempt to quell public unrest and growing opposition to the regime.

On April 2, Argentine forces took control of Port Stanley, the capital of the Falkland Islands, in the South Atlantic. The next day, they also seized South Georgia and the South Sandwich Islands by force.

The Falkland Islands (as they are known in the United Kingdom) or the Malvinas (as they are called in Argentina) lie about 310 miles from Argentina. Their sovereignty has been disputed since the nineteenth century. Argentina exercised sovereignty from 1820 to January 1833, when the United Kingdom expelled the Argentine authorities and the island's inhabitants.

Negotiations between Argentina and the United Kingdom over control of the islands—underway since 1960—were interrupted. Tensions had escalated further since 1976, during the dictatorship. The junta, appealing to long-standing patriotic claims, believed that recovering the Malvinas would unite Argentines and restore the regime's legitimacy. At first, thousands of people gathered in Plaza de Mayo, before the Casa Rosada, to express their support. But the momentum did not last.

The British response was swift and overwhelming. They mobilized all available forces to retake the islands, accomplishing this goal on June 14. The conflict had lasted seventy-four days and cost the lives of more than 900 people—650 Argentines and 255 British. Three days after the defeat, Galtieri resigned as commander-in-chief of the Army and as president.

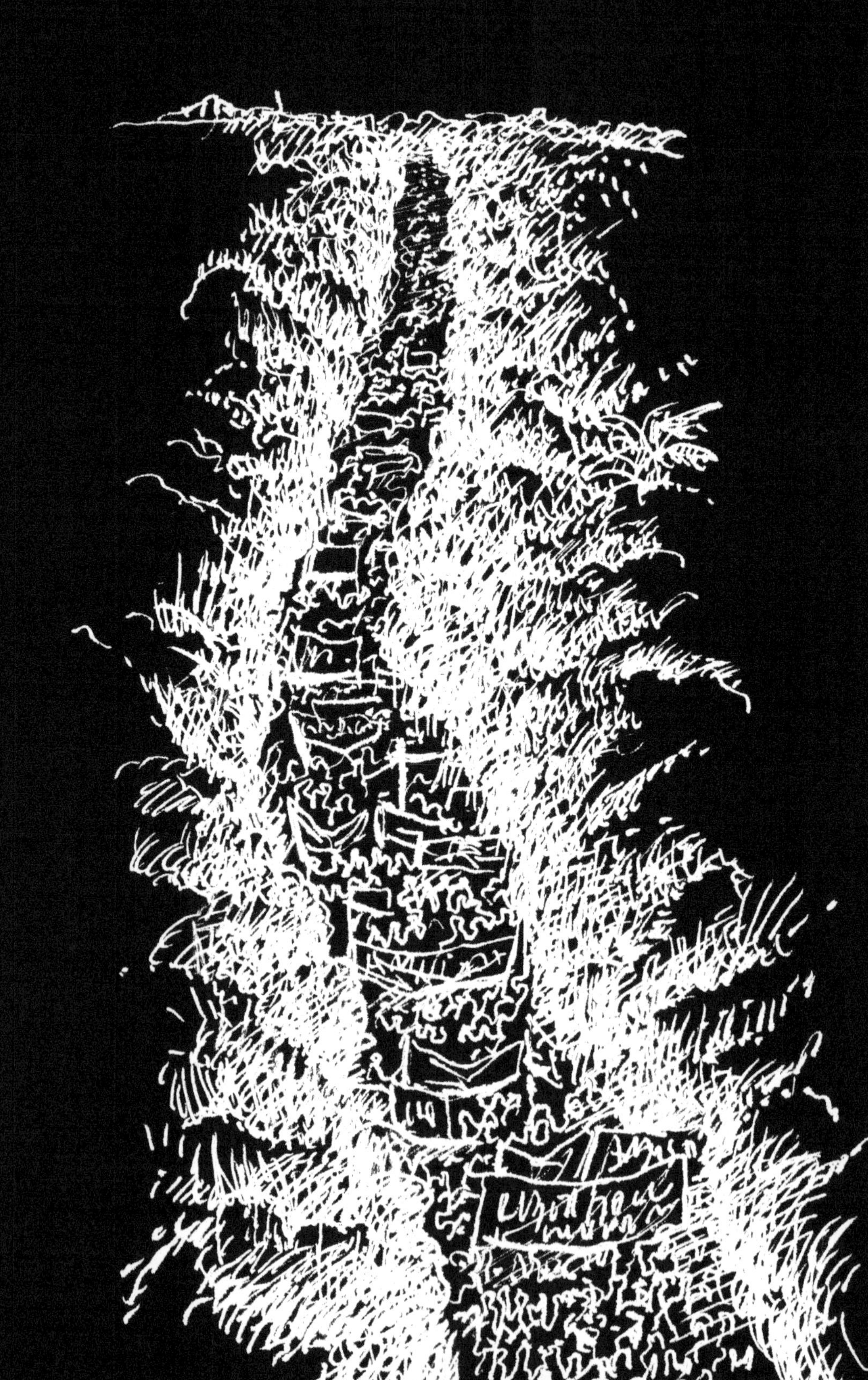

8. THE RETURN *of* DEMOCRACY

The winds of change began to blow in the 1980s, and the return to democracy loomed on the horizon across South America. Bolivia was the first country to undergo a democratic transition, in 1982. Argentina, Uruguay, Brazil, Paraguay, and finally Chile followed.

The return to democracy in South America took place during the so-called "third wave of democratization." U.S. political scientist Samuel Huntington coined the term to describe the wave of democratization processes that swept the globe, beginning with the 1974 Carnation Revolution in Portugal, and eventually encompassed more than 60 countries in Europe, Latin America, and Africa.

In the 1980s and 1990s, the first democratic governments faced enormous challenges. One of the most difficult was striking a balance between consolidating the newly recovered—yet still fragile—democratic institutions and responding to the demands for truth and justice from victims, their relatives, and human rights groups.

Different dynamics unfolded across the region. In most countries, the dictatorships had tightly controlled the transition processes, constraining the new governments from the outset through agreements and negotiations. The only exception was Argentina, where the dictatorship had imploded following the disastrous defeat in the Falklands War in 1982. That collapse worsened an already volatile mix of economic recession, revelations of previously unheard-of atrocities, and growing demands from politicians, trade unions, and the press.

In Argentina, a lawyer who had represented political prisoners during the dictatorship became the first democratically elected president in 1983. From the start, he charted a pioneering path in the region through his efforts to pursue truth and justice.

In contrast, Brazil, Paraguay, and Uruguay elected presidents who came from political parties with close ties to the armed forces. In Chile, although a center-left coalition won the election, Pinochet remained commander-in-chief of the Army until 1998, closely monitoring all that happened in the country.

BOLIVIA

Date of return to democracy: October 10, 1982
President: Hernán Siles Zuazo (Unidad Democrática y Popular; Democratic and Popular Unity)

ARGENTINA

Date of return to democracy: December 10, 1983
President: Raúl Alfonsín (Unión Cívica Radical; Radical Civic Union)

URUGUAY

Date of return to democracy: March 1, 1985
President: Julio María Sanguinetti (Partido Colorado; Colorado Party)

BRAzIL

Date of return to democracy: March 15, 1985
President: Tancredo Neves (president) and José Sarney (vice-president), of the Partido do Movimento Democrático Brasileiro (Party of the Brazilian Democratic Movement), won the 1985 elections. Hours before taking office, on March 15, Neves was hospitalized and died on April 21. His vice-president, José Sarney, assumed the presidency.

PARAGUAY

Date of return to democracy: February 3, 1989
President: General Andrés Rodríguez (Partido Colorado; Colorado Party)

CAM

NO
NO
NO
NO
NO

CHILE

Date of return to democracy: March 11, 1990
President: Patricio Aylwin Azócar (Concertación de Partidos por la Democracia; Coalition of Parties for Democracy)

9. JUSTICE *or* IMPUNITY?

In the early 1980s, Argentina's first democratically elected president after the dictatorship, Raúl Alfonsín, implemented unprecedented measures to investigate the crimes committed during those dark years. Just five days after taking office, on December 15, 1983, his government enacted Decree 187, establishing the pioneering National Commission on the Disappearance of Persons (CONADEP).

The CONADEP's main purpose was to clarify and investigate the forced disappearances that had occurred under military rule. Thirteen influential members, including Monsignor Jaime de Nevares, Rabbi Marshall T. Meyer, and journalist Magdalena Ruiz Guiñazú, composed the commission. Over nine months, it gathered thousands of testimonies from survivors, relatives, and other witnesses. It also identified and inspected clandestine detention and torture centers, burial sites, morgues, hospitals, and jails.

In September 1984, writer Ernesto Sábato—who presided over the CONADEP—delivered the final report *Nunca Más* (Never Again) to President Alfonsín. The report acknowledged the systematic and planned nature of human rights violations throughout Argentina. The CONADEP was the first truth commission in the world to complete its investigation and issue a final report, drawing international attention.

Three days after assuming the presidency, on December 13, 1983, Alfonsín had also signed Decree 158, ordering the prosecution of the military commanders who had led the first three juntas of the dictatorship.

Initially, the trial was held before the Supreme Council of the Armed Forces. But in September 1984, the council concluded that the acts of repression were "unobjectionable." As a result, the case was transferred to the Federal Court of Appeals in Buenos Aires in October. The so-called Trial of the Military Juntas—led by District Attorney Julio César Strassera and his aide Luis Moreno Ocampo—

took place before the six judges of the Court of Appeals from April to December 1985.

The court heard 839 witnesses, and they used the *Nunca Más* report as evidence.

On December 9, 1985, the Court sentenced former dictators Jorge Videla and Eduardo Massera to life imprisonment for homicide, unlawful detention, and torture. Three other military commanders received lighter sentences—between four and 17 years—while four were acquitted. In 1986, the Supreme Court ratified the verdict.

With the return to democracy, the relentless search by the mothers and grandmothers of disappeared—which had begun during the dictatorships—became a cry that no one could ignore. "Where are they?" was the slogan that united thousands of families across South America in their demand to uncover what had happened to their relatives during the years of state terrorism.

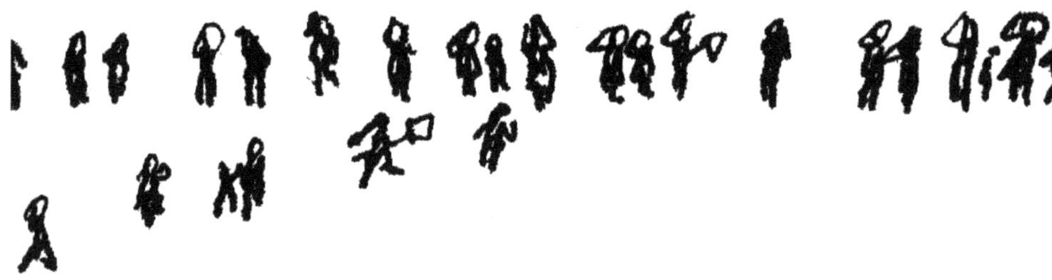

Soon, however, the pursuit of justice encountered obstacles in these new and fragile democracies.

The armed forces of the Southern Cone opposed the unfolding judicial proceedings, arguing that "the struggle against subversion" had been legitimate and that, "through their actions," they saved the homeland from "the communist threat."

In Argentina, after the Trial of the Juntas, activists and relatives of victims filed thousands of new lawsuits for human rights violations in 1986. This further inflamed discontent within the armed forces—the rattling of sabers began to echo from the barracks. The fragile democracies of the Southern Cone faced an untenable crossroads: justice or impunity?

The continued search for justice seemed to threaten the recently restored democratic life.

LEX

That winter in 1986, Chilean investigative journalist Mónica González traveled to Buenos Aires to investigate the murder of Chilean general Carlos Prats and his wife Sofía Cuthbert. Prats, who had been commander in chief of the Army until August 1973, went into exile in Buenos Aires after Pinochet's coup. Both were killed there on September 30, 1974, by a bomb placed under the general's car by DINA agent Michael Townley.

After knocking on many doors, González gained access to the five boxes of documents from the espionage trial that had followed DINA agent Enrique Arancibia Clavel's arrest in 1978. In that cold room of the Court Archive, she made a startling discovery: Arancibia Clavel's personal archive.

Arancibia Clavel had operated in Argentina from 1974 to 1978, and his files documented the repression carried out by the DINA beyond Chilean borders as part of the region's coordinated campaign. The journalist found memoranda he had regularly sent to his superiors in Santiago. The first is dated October 10, 1974; the last, October 12, 1978. All were signed with the pseudonym Luis Felipe Alamparte Díaz and addressed to Luis Gutiérrez, the alias used for whoever headed the DINA's Exterior Department.

By the late 1980s, the Southern Cone had turned toward impunity. Amid growing unrest within the armed forces, the Argentine Congress passed the Full Stop Law (Ley de Punto Final), enacted by President Alfonsín on December 24, 1986. The law ended investigations into dictatorship-era crimes for all defendants who had not been summoned to testify within 60 days of its promulgation. As a result, all legal proceedings would come to a halt. Over 50,000 people demonstrated against the law in Buenos Aires, in a protest called by the Mothers and Grandmothers of Plaza de Mayo.

Later, after the first uprising by a group of Argentine Army officers known as the carapintadas (painted faces) during Easter week in 1987, Congress approved a second impunity law on June 4. The Law of Due Obedience (Ley de Obediencia Debida) exonerated subordinate military officers for crimes committed while following orders from superiors.

Neighboring countries also passed similar impunity laws. In Uruguay, Parliament approved in December 1986 the Law on the Expiry of the Punitive Claims of the State (Ley de Caducidad de la Pretensión Punitiva del Estado), ensuring impunity for military and police officers. In Chile and Brazil, amnesty laws serving the same purpose had been enacted during the dictatorships themselves, in April 1978 and August 1979, respectively.

10. *The* SEARCH *for* TRUTH *and* JUSTICE

In the early 1990s, a mighty wall of impunity prevailed in the Southern Cone. In Argentina, after the impunity laws were enacted, President Carlos Menem pardoned hundreds of military officers under investigation between 1989 and 1990. This included the commanders who had received sentences during the Trial of the Juntas.

In an attempt to confront impunity, survivors, relatives, and human rights lawyers developed a new tactic for strategic litigation: using the courts of foreign countries to seek justice for dictatorship-era atrocities. Since many Argentine victims were descendants of European immigrants, their relatives could file criminal complaints in countries such as Spain, Germany, France, and Italy.

These efforts began to bear fruit in the 1990s. A criminal court in Paris sentenced Alfredo Astiz, a navy captain from the Navy School of Mechanics (ESMA), to life in prison in absentia for the kidnapping and murder of French nuns Alice Domon and Léonine Duquet in 1977. Prosecutors subsequently investigated and tried several other military officers, including former dictators Jorge Videla and Eduardo Massera.

The trials held outside South America were significant for two reasons. First, European courts investigated the crimes committed by South American dictatorships and delivered the justice long awaited by the victims and their relatives. Second, the unfolding of these foreign criminal proceedings strongly affected Argentina and directly helped reactivate local efforts toward justice. In effect, the prosecutions abroad pushed Argentine judges to reopen investigations into the dictatorship's crimes in their own courts.

In 1989, Paraguay also returned to democracy. The new democratic constitution which took effect in June 1992, granted citizens a novel right: habeas data. This allowed individuals to access information held by the state about themselves.

Seizing this opportunity, educationalist and human rights activist Martín Almada, a former political prisoner under the Stroessner dictatorship, filed a habeas data petition before the courts in September 1992. It was the first case of this type in the country and was assigned to Judge José Agustín Fernández. In the course of the investigation, the Paraguayan police initially responded that no documents related to Almada, claiming they had disappeared in February 1989 during the coup d'état.

Thanks to information later leaked from within the police, Almada and Judge Fernández met at the Directorate of Production of the Capital Police in Lambaré, in the outskirts of Asunción, on December 22, 1992. The judge ordered the deputy superintendent to let them in. Following the information in Almada's possession, they discovered a room in a sealed off part of the building whose door they had to force open. Inside, they found a six-foot-tall pile containing thousands of documents. Other records were found buried in the patio. The documents had likely been taken there in haste, with no time to destroy them.

The documents discovered by Almada and Judge Fernández became known as the "Archives of Terror." Produced between 1930 and 1992 and comprising around 700,000 pages, many of these documents date from the Stroessner dictatorship (1954-1989).

The records came from the Investigations Department of the Capital Police, the National Directorate of Technical Affairs, and the Ministry of the Interior. Among them were files on detained individuals, interrogation reports, prisoner entry and exit records, intelligence reports on persons and organizations, audiotapes, and photographs.

One of the records found was a report sent by Superintendent Alberto Cantero to Pastor Coronel, chief of the Investigations Department of the Capital Police, on May 16, 1977. The document recorded the handover of Uruguayan and Argentine prisoners Gustavo Inzaurralde, Nelson Santana, José Luis Nell, Alejandro Logoluso, and Dora Landi to two agents of the intelligence service of the Argentine Army. The five were flown to Buenos Aires.

DPTO. DE INVESTIGAC.
DIREC. DE POLITICA
Y AFINES.-
-oOo-

00172F 0098

Asunción, 16 de Mayo de 1.977.-

OBJETO : Elevar informe

AL : Sr.Jefe del III Dpto.de Investigaciones
Don PASTOR MILCIADES CORONEL
E. S. D.-

Tengo el honor de dirigirme a esa superioridad, con el objeto de elevar a su conocimiento que en el día de la fecha, siendo las 16.34 horas, en un avión Bi-reactor de la Armada Argentina, con matricula 5-7-30 - 0653, piloteado por el Capitán de Corbeta JOSE ABDALA, viajaron con destino a la ciudad de Buenos Aires(R.A.), los siguientes detenidos: GUSTAVO EDISON INSAURRALDE (uruguayo, NELSON RODOLFO SANTANA SCOTTO (uruguayo), JOSE NELL (argentino), ALEJANDRO JOSE LOGOLUSO (argentino) y DORA MARTA LANDI GIL (argentina). Las mencionadas personas fueren entregadas por conducto de esta Dirección, en presencia del Cnel.D.E.M. Don BENITO GUANES y del Cap. de Fragata LAZARO SOSA, al Tte.1º JOSE MON

Crio. Insp. OP. Alberto B. Cantero
DIRECTOR DE POLITICA Y AFINES

Asunción, 16 de Mayo de 1.977.-

A conocimiento del Señor Jefe de Policía.-

Pastor M. Coronel
JEFE III DPTO. DE INVESTIGACIONES

In Argentina during the 1990s, the only dictatorship-era crimes that continued to be prosecuted were those involving the unlawful appropriation of children—cases that fell outside the scope of the country's impunity laws. Between 1988 and 2005, twenty-three individuals were sentenced. But many more perpetrators remained free; it is estimated that there were approximately 500 cases of baby abduction.

In this context of institutional impunity, activists and human rights lawyers sought ingenious ways to achieve justice. In addition to pursuing trials abroad, a second strategic litigation tactic emerged: filing complaints in Argentine courts for crimes not covered by the impunity laws.

On December 30, 1996, four lawyers led by Alberto Pedroncini filed a complaint in the name of six Grandmothers of Plaza de Mayo—among them Estela de Carlotto and María Isabel Chorobik—alleging the existence of a Systematic Plan for the Unlawful Appropriation of Children. They argued that families loyal to the dictatorship had illegally adopted babies born to women held clandestine in detention, and that this constituted a coordinated, nationwide plan. The Trial of the Juntas in 1985 documented the abduction of minors, but it could not prove the countrywide organized manner of these abductions.

In 1998, several former high-ranking officials, including Videla and Massera, were indicted for baby theft, abduction, and falsification of identity.

By the late 1990s, a more favorable context for the struggle against impunity finally appeared on the horizon. In March 1998, the Argentine Congress repealed the impunity laws. They could no longer apply to new lawsuits, although they remained in effect for cases already filed.

On the other side of the Andes, important steps were being taken in Chile. In January 1998, relatives of disappeared and murdered victims filed two complaints in Santiago, accusing former General Augusto Pinochet himself—for the first time—of human rights violations during the dictatorship.

Months later, on October 16 of that year, Pinochet was placed under house arrest in London, where he had traveled for back surgery. The arrest was based on a warrant issued by Spanish judge Baltasar Garzón.

Judge Garzón sought to bring former General Pinochet to trial for the murders of several Spanish citizens during the Chilean dictatorship.

The Progressive Union of Prosecutors had filed the complaint in Spain on July 4, 1996, in Valencia. The next day, jurist Joan Garcés presented a criminal complaint on behalf of the victims in the National High Court (Audiencia Nacional). At that time, Spanish law allowed for universal jurisdiction, while in Chile, there was almost absolute impunity regarding the dictatorship's crimes.

The criminal case leading to Pinochet's arrest included charges of genocide, murder, and torture of 94 victims, with Operation Condor at its core. In the arrest warrant, Judge Garzón stated that Chilean and Argentine military officers had carried out coordinated criminal actions across several countries to physically eliminate, torture, kidnap, and disappear Chilean and foreign citizens.

Although the London court authorized the former dictator's extradition on October 15, 1999, on March 2, 2000, the Home Secretary, Jack Straw, released him on humanitarian grounds, citing his state of health. Nonetheless, during the 503 days of his detention in London, the number of complaints filed in Chile for dictatorship-era crimes grew exponentially. Upon his return, Chile forced Pinochet to face several criminal proceedings, including for crimes related to Operation Condor.

In May 1995, in Argentina, relatives of four victims with ties to the Center for Legal and Social Studies (CELS)—including its president, Emilio Mignone, and Carmen Aguiar de Lapacó—presented complaints before the Federal Court of Appeals in Buenos Aires. They invoked the emerging right to truth, seeking to uncover the circumstances of the disappearances of their respective daughters, Mónica Mignone and Alejandra Lapacó.

In October 1998, after Argentine courts had refused to investigate, Aguiar de Lapacó filed a petition before the Inter-American Commission on Human Rights. In November 1999, the commission mediated a friendly settlement: Argentina pledged to guarantee the right to truth and to employ all means necessary to clarify what had happened to the disappeared. Thus, the so-called "Truth Trials" were established, which combined features of criminal trials and truth commissions. They took place in the early 2000s in several Argentine provinces and cities, especially Buenos Aires and La Plata. This innovative process allowed victims and relatives to advance toward the truth, clarifying the facts and systematizing the information, even if those responsible could not be convicted.

Parallel to the lawsuits for baby abductions in Argentina, complaints were also filed for other crimes beyond the reach of the impunity laws: the atrocities of Operation Condor, which had occurred across multiple countries.

On November 8, 1999, lawyers Alberto Pedroncini and David Baigún filed a second key complaint in the struggle against impunity in Argentina. Supported by two other lawyers and the Permanent Assembly for Human Rights, the complaint that launched the Operation Condor case was filed on behalf of six women, who were relatives of victims: the Chilean Dora Carreño, the Paraguayan Idalina Radice, the Uruguayan Sara Méndez, and the Argentines Elsa Pavón, Claudia Careaga and Ana María Careaga.

Seven forced disappearances were denounced: those of Chilean Cristina Carreño, Paraguayans Federico Tatter and María Esther Ballestrino, Uruguayan Simón Riquelo (aged 21 days), and the Argentine couple Mónica Grinspón and Claudio Logares and their daughter Paula (aged two years). All had disappeared between 1976 and 1978 in Argentina and Uruguay.

The main charges were forced disappearance (unlawful deprivation of liberty) and criminal conspiracy. Seventeen high-ranking officers were accused of involvement in the creation of a cross-border criminal organization. Among them were former dictators Videla (Argentina), Pinochet (Chile), and Stroessner (Paraguay), as well as the commander of the Uruguayan Army, Julio César Vadora, and six Uruguayan agents who had operated in Automotores Orletti, including José Nino Gavazzo and Manuel Cordero.

Simón Riquelo

Cristina Carreño

Claudio Logares,
Mónica Grinspón
y Paula Eva Logares

María Esther Ballestrino

Federico Tatter

PB.

36 UNCLASSIFIED

DF001

DEPARTMENT OF STATE

E.O. 12065: N/A

7900091-0908

TAGS : SHUM AR DECONTROL

FROM: : Amembassy BUENOS AIRES

SUBJECT : Human Rights Case Reports

DATE : June 19, 1979

REF :

Between 1999 and 2000, in a more favorable global context for human rights, President Bill Clinton declassified thousands of documents of various US agencies—including the FBI, the CIA, and the State Department—related to Chile.

In 1995, Clinton had issued an executive order requiring US intelligence agencies to allow the declassification of documents produced twenty-five years earlier or more, provided they did not compromise nuclear secrets, intelligence sources and methods, and other national security concerns.

Among the declassified materials were documents referring to Operation Condor, the murder of former Chilean Foreign Minister Orlando Letelier and his US colleague Ronni Moffit in Washington in September 1976, as well as others containing information about victims of forced disappearance in Argentina, Brazil, Peru, and Bolivia.

In this increasingly favorable context for the search for truth, justice, and reparations in Argentina, archeological excavations began on April 13, 2020, in search of the remains of the clandestine detention center known as El Club Atlético (The Athletic Club).

In 2005, the Buenos Aires Legislature declared it a Historical Site, and in 2014 it was classified as a National Historical Site. Among other activities, the site offers guided tours, informational talks, and workshops for elementary and middle school students.

The archeological excavation was essential to recovering the site because, in late 1977, the building where the clandestine center had operated on Paseo Colón Avenue—in the San Telmo neighborhood—was demolished to make way for the construction of the new “25 de Mayo” highway. On December 28, 1977, authorities transferred the last prisoners held there to another secret jail known as El Banco, on Camino de Cintura and the Ricchieri highway in the province of Buenos Aires.

11. A RENEWED DRIVE *for* JUSTICE

After more than a decade of impunity in Argentina, an important political shift toward justice took place during the Néstor Kirchner administration (2003–2007). In August 2003, Congress repealed the Due Obedience and Full Stop laws.

Even before that, in its ongoing efforts to overcome impunity, the CELS had developed an innovative legal argument in the case of the abducted baby Claudia Poblete, which the Grandmothers of Plaza de Mayo had denounced in 1998. In late 2000, the CELS had requested the courts to investigate the torture and disappearance of her father and mother: José Poblete and Gertrudis Hlaczik. It also demanded that the courts declare the impunity laws unconstitutional. These laws put the courts in a contradictory position, as they allowed prosecution for the baby's kidnapping and identity alteration but not for the original crime of her parents' disappearance.

In March 2001, Federal Judge Gabriel Cavallo declared the impunity laws unconstitutional, affirming that they violated international law. The appeals court upheld the ruling in November. However, the unconstitutionality ruling applied only to this specific case.

The reopening of the trials occurred a few years later. In June 2005, the Supreme Court confirmed that the impunity laws were unconstitutional in the Poblete-Simón Case and ruled that this precedent was applicable to similar cases. The Court held—in line with the jurisprudence of the Inter-American Court of Human Rights in the 2001 Barrios Altos v. Peru case—that amnesty or impunity laws could not shield the dictatorship's crimes.

Nothing in President Kirchner's personal or political trajectory could have predicted his support for the struggle against impunity upon assuming the presidency in May 2003. Besides backing the repeal of the impunity laws, Kirchner—who presented himself as a son of the Mothers of Plaza de Mayo—took other important steps. On March 24, 2004, he ordered the removal of portraits of former dictators Videla and Bignone from the National Military College. That same day, the Navy received orders to vacate the ESMA building, and they later transformed it into a space for memory and the promotion of human rights. In August 2004, Congress passed a reparations law for minors who had been victims of state terrorism, including those whose identities had been stolen.

On the other side of the Andes, important advances were also underway in the search for justice and truth in Chile.

On September 7, 1999, Judge Juan Guzmán Tapia—who had been investigating the accusations against former dictator Pinochet since 1998—formally opened the Operation Condor case. This investigation had emerged as a result of the spontaneous complaints progressively filed by relatives of the victims.

After a failed attempt to prosecute Pinochet over the Caravan of Death episode in 2002, the judge once again sought to bring him to trial in late 2003, this time for the Operation Condor episode. Unexpectedly, in 2004, both the Court of Appeals and the Supreme Court backed the judge's request and authorized prosecuting Pinochet for the crimes of Operation Condor. On December 13, 2004, Guzmán Tapia indicted Pinochet for nine kidnappings and one murder of Chilean victims forcibly disappeared between 1975 and 1977 in Paraguay, Bolivia, and Argentina.

As criminal trials gradually started to take place in the early 2000s across the Southern Cone, several police and military officers involved in state terrorism fled their home countries to avoid justice.

Former Uruguayan military intelligence colonel Manuel Cordero escaped to Brazil in 2004 to avoid a complaint filed against him for glorifying the crime of torture. A few months later, in January 2005, Brazilian human rights activist Jair Krischke and Uruguayan investigative journalist Roger Rodríguez tracked him down: he had moved to the border city of Santana do Livramento, in the Brazilian state of Rio Grande do Sul.

Cordero was finally arrested in February 2007 when he went to the Uruguayan consulate to sign a power of attorney allowing his brother-in-law to collect his pension in Uruguay. After a lengthy legal process, he was extradited to Argentina in January 2010, enabling his prosecution for 11 cases of abductions carried out during Operation Condor.

The struggle against impunity also began to bear fruit in Uruguay. On September 17, 2010, criminal judge Mariana Mota ordered the imprisonment of retired military intelligence colonel Carlos Calcagno for his participation in the disappearance of Gustavo Inzaurralde and Nelson Santana in Paraguay.

It was a historic indictment: Mota became the first Uruguayan magistrate to charge the crime of forced disappearance as defined by international law—a definition established in Uruguay through Law 18,026 of 2006, which ratified the Rome Statute of the International Criminal Court. In doing so, the judge accepted prosecutor Mirtha Guianze's request.

In July 2011, the Court of Appeals upheld Mota's indictment and confirmed that forced disappearance constitutes a continuing crime.

On April 26, 2011, Paraguay declared the former Investigations Department of the Capital Police a Historic and Memory Site. The Ministry of the Interior and the Interinstitutional Commission for the Establishment and Implementation of the Network of Historic and Memory Sites of Paraguay promoted the designation.

During the Stroessner dictatorship, the Investigations Department planned and executed the regime's political repression. Its jurisdiction extended not only across the entire Paraguayan territory but also beyond the country's borders through the collaborative framework of Operation Condor.

July 5, 2012, became a historic date in the pursuit of justice in Argentina. On that day, a court in Buenos Aires delivered the verdict in the legal case known as the Systematic Plan, which investigated 34 cases of child appropriation carried out during the dictatorship. Federal Oral Court n. 6, presided over by Judge María del Carmen Roqueta, sentenced former dictator Jorge Videla to 50 years in prison. The court recognized that between 1976 and 1983, the dictatorship's security forces systematically abducted, retained, and concealed children under the age of 10 while their mothers were secretly imprisoned.

The judges convicted eight other defendants—including former dictator Reynaldo Bignone and Jorge "El Tigre" Acosta, head of ESMA's Task Force 3.3.2. This case had been filed in late 1996 by lawyer Pedroncini on behalf of the Grandmothers of Plaza de Mayo.

¿DONDE
CENTE
NACIDOS

AN, LOS
S DE BEBES
CAUTIVERIO ?
UELAS DE PZA DE MAYO

The ruling in the case concerning the systematic plan of child appropriation represented a milestone in the long struggle of the Grandmothers of Plaza de Mayo, who since 1977 had tirelessly demanded the return of their grandchildren abducted during the period of state terrorism. The verdict encompassed the cases of 34 children who were born in or taken from various clandestine detention centers, including the 5th Police Station in the city of La Plata, the Campo de Mayo military base, ESMA, and Automotores Orletti.

Nine of the cases involved children of victims detained during Operation Condor. These included Macarena Gelman, granddaughter of Argentine poet Juan Gelman, who was born in early November 1976 while her mother, María Claudia García Iruretagoyena, was held captive in Montevideo; and Anatole and Victoria Julien, children of Uruguayan exiles who were kidnapped with their parents in San Martín, province of Buenos Aires, on September 26, 1976, and later abandoned in late December 1976 in Valparaíso, Chile, after also spending time imprisoned in Uruguay.

The struggle of the Grandmothers of Plaza de Mayo continues to this day, including at the international level through a campaign for the Right to Identity undertaken together with Argentina's Ministry of Foreign Affairs and the National Commission for the Right to Identity. Thanks to their indefatigable efforts, as of July 2025, the Grandmothers have resolved the cases of 140 grandchildren (out of an estimated total of at least 500 cases).

12. OPERATION CONDOR TRIAL *in* ARGENTINA

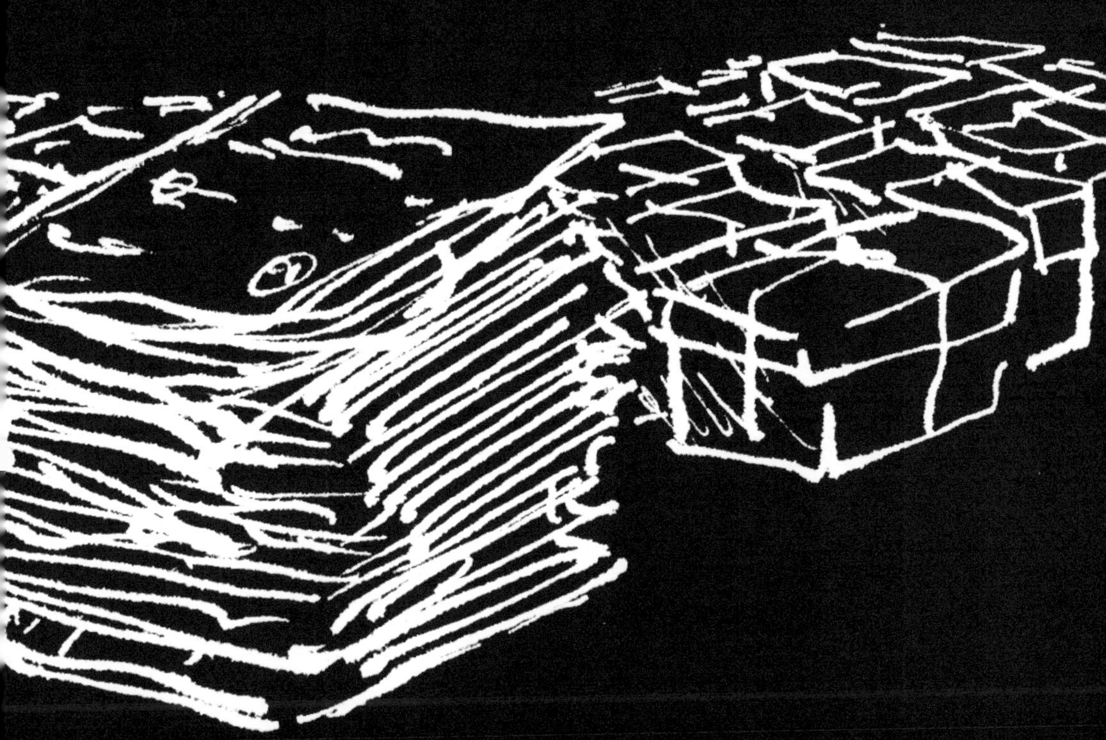

5/3/2013

With the reopening of criminal proceedings in 2005 for crimes committed during Argentina's dictatorship, several legal cases that had been filed years earlier finally reached the stage of oral and public trial. One such case was Operation Condor and Automotores Orletti II, whose trial began on March 5, 2013, in Buenos Aires after nearly fifteen years of investigation. Lawyer Pedroncini and his colleagues had filed the original complaint in late 1999.

The trial took place before the Federal Oral Court n. 1 in Buenos Aires, presided by Judges Oscar Ricardo Amirante, Adrián Federico Grünberg, Pablo Gustavo Laufer, and substitute judge Ricardo Ángel Basílico.

The case had grown exponentially since 1999. With the inclusion of three Operation Condor files and one Orletti case file, the total number of victims reached 173 and defendants 27, an increase from the seven victims and 17 defendants reported in 1999. Among the defendants were a Uruguayan officer, Manuel Cordero, and 26 Argentines, with 24 from the Army, one from the Navy, and one from the State Intelligence Secretariat (SIDE). The list included symbolic figures of Argentina's dictatorship, such as former dictator Reynaldo Bignone (1982–1983), the commander of the Fourth Army Corps, Santiago Riveros, and the head of the Battalion of Engineers 181 in Neuquén, Enrique Olea.

Twenty-five defendants were tried as indirect perpetrators—meaning they held decision-making positions and gave the orders—for illegal kidnappings and criminal conspiracy. By contrast, Cordero and SIDE agent Miguel Ángel Furci were charged as direct perpetrators for personally carrying out kidnappings and acts of torture. Prosecutors could only prosecute Cordero for 11 kidnappings because of his extradition terms from Brazil. In contrast, in the Orletti II case, Furci was charged with abduction and torture making him the sole defendant in this regard.

The judges had to investigate the cases of 173 victims: 67 in Orletti II and 106 in the three files of the Operation Condor investigation. The latter comprised 47 Uruguayans, 21 Chileans, 17 Argentines, 11 Paraguayans, nine Bolivians, and one Peruvian.

Jorge Rafael Videla

Exp. Nº 13.445/99

CAUSA 1504

Humberto José Lobaiza

exp. 2510/08

CAUSA 1951

EXPEDIENTE Nº 13.445/1999
↓
CAUSA Nº 1.054
"PLAN CÓNDOR I"

EXPEDIENTE Nº 2.510 /200
↓
CAUSA Nº 1.951
"PLAN CÓNDOR

Nestor Horacio
Falcón
Exp. 10.961/11
Causa 2.054

Miguel Ángel
Furci
exp. 2.637/04
Causa 1.976

EXPEDIENTE
Nº 10.961/2011
↓
CAUSA Nº
2.054
"PLAN CÓNDOR III"

EXPEDIENTE
Nº 2.637/2004

CAUSA Nº
1.976
"ORLETTI II"

Judges:

Oscar Ricardo Amirante
Adrián Federico Grünberg
Pablo Gustavo Laufer
Ricardo Ángel Basílico (substitute)

Location:

Federal Oral Court n. 1 of the Federal Capital (Argentina)

Duration: 3 years, 2 months, and 22 days

Victims:

106 in the cases Operation Condor I, II, and III
67 in the case of Automotores Orletti II

Witnesses:

222 individuals

Case titles from the court's registry:

"Videla, Jorge Rafael and others – illegal deprivation of personal liberty"
"Lobaiza, Humberto José Román and others – illegal deprivation of liberty [...]"
"Falcón, Néstor Horacio and others – criminal conspiracy and illegal deprivation of liberty"
"Furci, Miguel Ángel – aggravated illegal deprivation of liberty and infliction of torture"

Public prosecutors:

Pablo Ouviña (chief prosecutor)
María Mercedes Moguilansky (ad hoc prosecutor)

Private prosecutors:

Jaime Nuguer (original lawsuit)
Luz Palmás Zaldua (unified lawsuit by CELS, Kaos Legal Team, Argentine Human Rights League, and attorney Alcira Ríos)
Alejandro Rúa
Martín Rico (Secretariat of Human Rights)

Defense attorneys:

Gerardo Ibáñez
María Laura Olea
Valeria Atienza
Federico Malato
José Soaje Pinto
Pamela Bisserier
Sergio Steizel
Nicolás Méstola
Carlos Gutiérrez
Eduardo San Emeterio
Carlos Meira
Mariano Meira

For the Operation Condor and Automotores Orletti II trial, the Argentine court gathered and systematized the largest collection of evidence ever compiled about the crimes committed during the coordinated repression in South America. Through a truly titanic and unprecedented effort, the judges cross-referenced academic research, thousands of archival documents, and hundreds of testimonies of survivors and experts. The documentation comprised 100,000 pages and more than 106 boxes.

In order to deliver a verdict, the court was also forced to cross borders—both symbolically and in practice—gathering all pertinent and necessary evidence from across the region and beyond. Crimes committed in six countries were investigated—Argentina, Brazil, Bolivia, Chile, Paraguay, and Uruguay, resulting in both Argentine and Uruguayan perpetrators. It was the trial of Operation Condor itself.

Two months after the beginning of the trial, on May 17, 2013, former dictator Videla died in prison. His death had both significant symbolic impact and important legal consequences. In the Operation Condor trial, Videla was one of the most relevant defendants accused of the transnational criminal conspiracy and the only one indicted for the disappearance of 44 victims.

It was ultimately decided that all crimes attributed to Videla would continue to be investigated to uphold the victims' right to truth—and also because the charge of criminal conspiracy involved a series of interrelated offenses. However, when the trial concluded, the court could not sentence anyone for those 44 disappearances, as only the former dictator faced accusations for them.

The prosecution team was led by Prosecutor General Pablo Ouviña, ad hoc prosecutor María Mercedes Moguilansky, and secretary Santiago Ghiglione. The nine-person team was multidisciplinary, including historian Melisa Slatman from the University of Buenos Aires, who examined the thousands of archive documents analyzed in the trial.

The prosecutors had three main objectives:

1. To uncover the truth.
2. To ensure that the perpetrators faced penal consequences for their crimes.
3. To provide answers to the victims and their relatives.

Between August and November 2015, the prosecutors presented their closing arguments to the court, recounting the background, scope, and actions carried out in South America during Operation Condor. In particular, they stated that Operation Condor was a criminal organization composed of states that coordinated their structures and resources, to commit the most serious crimes against humanity. They further argued that the operation had standardized preexisting practices of regional coordination to implement them at a higher level and that it had established an innovative framework to facilitate both bilateral and multilateral regional cooperation.

“We combined academic, historical, and journalistic research with documentary sources and, of course, witness statements:

the documentation and the historical works would have been incomplete without living testimonies. That was the true novelty in this trial."

JUEZ ADRIÁN FEDERICO GRÜNBERG

Documents from U.S. and South American archives—among them the memoranda by Chilean agent Arancibia Clavel—played a central role in corroborating the existence of Operation Condor. Expert witnesses like Rosa Palau (from Paraguay's Archives of Terror), Verónica Almada (from Argentina's Ministry of Defense), and Claudia Bellingeri (from the Provincial Commission for Memory of La Plata) testified before the judges and helped unravel the inner workings of the coordinated repression.

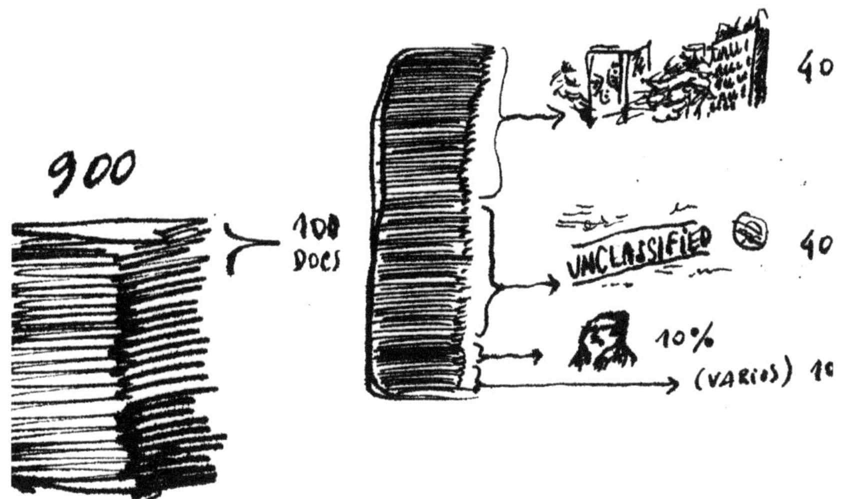

In March 2015, Carlos Osorio, director of the Southern Cone Documentation Project of the U.S. NGO National Security Archive, testified for more than 11 hours before the judges. He scrutinized nearly one hundred documents—out of the 900 he officially submitted—containing key evidence for the cases examined during the trial.

At 5:00 pm on May 27, 2016, after more than 38 months of hearings, the first-instance verdict was read, closing this historic trial. It was an unprecedented sentence in the struggle for justice for the atrocities committed by the coordinated repression in South America.

The presiding judge, Oscar Ricardo Amirante, read the resolution, which sentenced 14 Argentine defendants and one Uruguayan accused of the kidnappings and torture suffered by the victims. The defendants were also condemned for creating a transnational criminal conspiracy dedicated to perpetrating human rights violations across borders—in other words, for participating in Operation Condor.

On the day of the sentencing, hundreds of survivors, relatives of the victims, and journalists filled four courtrooms on Comodoro Py Avenue, in downtown Buenos Aires—they had specially prepared two of these to accommodate the large audience. Argentine embassies and consulates in Santiago de Chile, Asunción, Porto Alegre, Lima, São Paulo, and Montevideo also broadcast the reading of the verdict live. Major international media outlets published reports on the sentences, including *The New York Times, The Washington Post*, and the BBC, the next day.

In 2016, a first instance ruling definitively determined that South American criminal states established in the mid-1970s a network facilitating widespread cross-border human rights abuses against their citizens, spreading immense terror regionally and internationally. The judges determined that this secretly organized and coordinated alliance among repressive forces was indeed a vast transnational criminal conspiracy

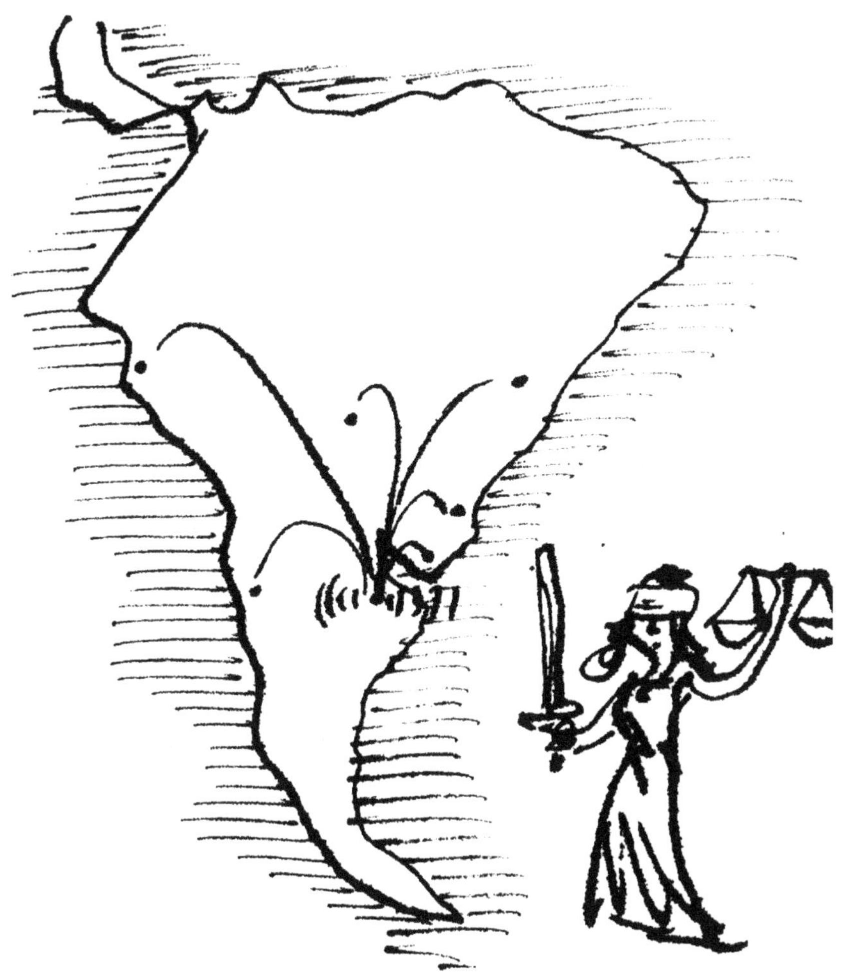

Of the 27 defendants:

15 were sentenced (14 Argentine military officers* and the Uruguayan Cordero).

Two were absolved.
Six died during the trial.
Four were deemed unfit to stand trial.

* Among the fourteen Argentines sentenced was the former Commander of Navy Operations, retired Admiral Antonio Vañek. He was sentenced to 13 years in prison for his participation in the kidnapping of Gustavo Inzaurralde.

First-instance sentences (2016)

1. Santiago Omar Riveros (Army), 25 years in prison.
2. Miguel Ángel Furci (SIDE), 25 years.
3. Reynaldo Benito Bignone (Army), 20 years.
4. Eduardo Samuel de Lío (Army), 12 years.
5. Humberto José Román Lobaiza ((Army), 18 years.
6. Enrique Braulio Olea (Army), 13 years.
7. Luis Sadi Pepa (Army), 12 years.
8. Rodolfo Emilio Feroglio Army), 20 years.
9. Carlos Caggiano Tedesco (Army), 12 years.
10. Antonio Vañek (Navy), 13 years.
11. Eugenio Guañabens Perelló (Army), 13 years.
12. Felipe Jorge Alespeiti (Army), 12 years.
13. Manuel Cordero Piacentini (Uruguayan Army), 25 years.
14. Néstor Horacio Falcón (Army), 12 years.
15. Federico Antonio Minicucci (Army), eight years.
16. Juan Avelino Rodríguez (Army), absolved.
17. Carlos Tragant (Army), absolved.

On May 4, 2018, Chamber IV of the Federal Court of Criminal Cassation, presided over by Judge Mariano Hernán Borinsky, rejected the appeals and unconstitutionality challenges filed by the defendants' attorneys, upholding the first-instance sentences.

By October 2025, the Supreme Court dismissed all the pending appeals and ratified all the sentences against the convicted individuals.

LEX
Igualdad

LEX
la Ley.

OPEN EPILOGUE

The struggle for truth, justice, and reparations for the crimes of Operation Condor continues. In the research carried out for the collaborative project plancondor.org, we mapped the judicial cases that, since the 1970s, have investigated the crimes perpetrated by the repressive coordination in South America.

As of March 2026, there were 50 criminal cases in the courts of nine countries: Argentina, Brazil, Chile, the United States, France, Italy, Paraguay, Peru, and Uruguay. At least one first-instance sentence was issued in 40 cases; three are now in the trial stage (oral or written), four are still under investigation; and three have been dismissed.

The country with the largest number of investigations is Uruguay (17 cases), followed by Argentina (14), Chile (8), and Italy (6). These criminal proceedings are scrutinizing the cases of 461 victims, and the crimes under investigation are mainly kidnappings, homicides, and torture. Out of 805 victims of the coordinated repression between 1969 and 1981, the majority were nationals of Uruguay (48%), Argentina (23%), and Chile (14%). They were predominantly political and social activists (40%), and members of guerrilla groups (36%).

The judicialization of Operation Condor's atrocities has been possible, above all, because of the tireless efforts of survivors, relatives, activists, human rights lawyers, journalists, justice professionals, and scholars. These justice seekers have had to cross borders and overcome many obstacles along the way to gather the evidence necessary for these Condor trials. On the pages that follow, we detail some of the latest progress in justice, truth, and reparation.

In Italy, on July 9, 2021, the Supreme Court of Cassation—the country's highest court—upheld the life sentences of 11 former Uruguayan officers and three Chileans convicted of murder in the Operation Condor trial in Rome.

In June 1999, when impunity still prevailed in the Southern Cone, five Uruguayan women and one Argentine—represented by Italian lawyer Giancarlo Maniga—filed lawsuits before the Rome Prosecutor's Office regarding the homicides of their relatives, who were Italian citizens. Former Uruguayan Navy Captain Jorge Néstor Tróccoli—the only convicted person living in Italy after fleeing from Uruguay in 2007 to escape justice—was arrested on July 10, 2021, and transferred to prison to begin serving his life sentence.

A year later, on July 14, 2022, preliminary hearings began before the Third Assize Court in Rome in a second trial for victims of Operation Condor. Tróccoli, already serving a life sentence for 26 homicides, was now called to answer for the murders of three more victims:

Rafaela Giuliana Filipazzi, Italian, 33 years old when she was kidnapped on May 27, 1977, at the Hermitage Hotel in Montevideo.

José Agustín Potenza, Argentine, former Peronist militant, musician, 49 years old when he was arrested with his partner, Rafaela.

Elena Quinteros, Uruguayan, PVP militant, teacher, 30 years old at the time of her abduction in Montevideo on June 24, 1976.

This second trial began in 2019 when Italian lawyer Andrea Speranzoni and his colleague Alicia Mejía—who had traveled to Uruguay in 2018 to search for new evidence for the appeal stage of the Condor trial—found relevant documents not only for the ongoing trial but also to file another complaint.

Prosecutor Erminio Amelio took over the investigation after the Rome Prosecutor's Office received the evidence, which included the detention records of the three victims found in the archive of the Naval Fusiliers Corps (FUSNA) in Montevideo. Quinteros is still missing. In 2013, investigators found the remains of Filipazzi and Potenza in a mass grave on the premises of the Specialized Group of the National Police of Paraguay. The Capital Police had transferred the two victims to Asunción by plane in June 1977. Argentine forensic investigators identified the remains in 2016.

Despite Pinochet's death in 2006, the criminal investigation into the Condor episode in Chile continued with new defendants. The court released the appeal sentence on July 25, 2022. 22 former DINA agents were convicted for their roles in seven kidnappings and five homicides of Chilean victims during the coordinated Condor repression, as the Court of Appeals of Santiago, comprising Ministers Jessica González, Loreto Gutiérrez, and Jaime Balmaceda, altered the initial 2018 sentences.

The appellate court also significantly increased the prison sentences of some defendants—especially the high-ranking DINA officials Pedro Espinoza Bravo and Raúl Iturriaga Neumann. Additionally, for the first time, the judges accepted requests for symbolic reparations demanded by a relative, namely the acquisition of human rights books and the establishment of the Alexei Jaccard Siegler Award—named after one of the victims—for students at the University of Concepción.

In December 2023, the Supreme Court of Chile ratified the sentences of all agents.

In the context of the investigation of the Condor episode, the fate of some of the victims of the trans-Andean operations described in Chapter 4 was revealed. For decades, mystery shrouded their destiny. Only 30 years later, in 2007, did three former DINA agents confess before Chilean judge Víctor Montiglio that Jaccard, Ramírez, and Velásquez had been taken to the clandestine jail known as the Simón Bolívar Barracks, in the La Reina neighborhood of Santiago, where the agents murdered them two months later.

In 2015, investigators identified human remains discovered in the Cuesta Barriga mine—on the outskirts of Santiago, where the DINA regularly disposed of victims' bodies—as the couple Stoulman–Pessa and Ramírez. It was thus proven beyond doubt that these individuals, originally detained in Argentina, had been murdered in Chile as part of Operation Condor.

Alexei Vladimir
Jaccard Siegler

Ricardo Ignacio
Ramírez Herrera

Héctor Heraldo
Velásquez Mardones

Jacobo
Stoulman Bortnik

Matilde
Pessa Mois

Hernán Soto
Gálvez

Ruiter Enrique
Correa Arce

¿7 = T?

In the winter of 2022, in Montevideo, Uruguayan-Argentine artist Sebastián Santana was working on Cinco en Asunción (Five in Asunción), the last of three audiovisual productions to be released on the plancondor.org website—all created together with Pincho Casanova and Macarena Montañez, from the Pozodeagua Producing company, and musician Diego Presa. The making of this piece, which tells the story of five victims (Alejandro Logoluso, Dora Marta Landi, José Luis Nell, Gustavo Inzaurralde, and Nelson Santana), led to an entirely unexpected finding.

Sebastián wanted to draw as accurately as possible the plane used to transport the group of kidnapped victims between Asunción and Buenos Aires. He began searching for images of the plane online, starting with the aircraft's registration number, which was mentioned in a document from the Archives of Terror in Paraguay.

On July 29, surprisingly, he located the Hawker Siddeley HS-125 airplane: its registration number was actually 5T-30 (and not 5-7-30, as stated in the Paraguayan record—probably a transcription error, as confirmed by research conducted by the Argentine Anabel Alcaide and Uruguayan Samuel Blixen). Even more extraordinary was the fact that the plane had been i n Montevideo since 2008, at the Ángel S. Adami International Airport in Melilla, less than 20 kilometers from Sebastián's home. Something that no one had discovered until that moment.

Thousands of miles away from Uruguay, on February 14, 2023, hearings began in Rome in the second trial against Tróccoli. Francesca Lessa, an Italian researcher and at the time a lecturer at the University of Oxford, was the first to be heard by the magistrates, presided over by Judge Antonella Capri. That day, Francesca testified for more than three hours, explaining to the court the wave of military coups in South America, the policies of state terrorism implemented by the regimes, and the workings of Operation Condor.

She also provided details about the three victims—Rafaela Giuliana Filipazzi, José Agustín Potenza, and Elena Quinteros: their life trajectories, their paths of political militancy, and the events surrounding their abductions in Montevideo in 1976 and 1977—as well as about the accused, Tróccoli, who was serving at the time as the S-2 Intelligence Chief of the FUSNA.

In October 2025, Rome's Third Assize Court sentenced Tróccoli to life imprisonment for the three murders of Filipazzi, Potenza, and Quinteros.

Nearly a year after the plane's discovery in Montevideo, and following Sebastián Santana's public disclosure of its existence and location, Argentine lawyers Rodolfo Yanzón and Flavia Fernández Brozzi filed complaints in April 2023 before three federal courts in Argentina. The aircraft is relevant to the Condor Case, the ABO Circuit Case (which includes the clandestine centers Club Atlético, Banco, and Olimpo), and the ESMA Case. This lawsuit resulted from coordinated efforts by activists and human rights advocates in Uruguay and Argentina, especially Virginia Martínez in Montevideo and Graciela Daleo in Buenos Aires.Following this request, several developments took place. Argentine Judge Sebastián Casanello, who oversaw the Condor Case, took Santana's testimony in June 2023 to ratify the finding. He then asked the Uruguayan judiciary to take measures to preserve the aircraft—a request assigned to the Organized Crime Court of the 2nd Circuit, headed by Judge María Helena Mainard. Mainard ordered a precautionary measure and commissioned an expert report, which officially confirmed that the plane found in Melilla was the aircraft used for the victims' clandestine transportation. After receiving this confirmation, Casanello again contacted the Uruguayan judiciary, this time requesting cooperation to repatriate the aircraft. The request was accepted in April 2024.

The final step in this process–bringing the plane to Argentina– now depends on the Argentine government, which appears unlikely given President Javier Milei's administration and its reactionary stance on human rights.

The plane, which in 1977 was used exclusively to transport the Commander-in-Chief of the Argentine Navy, Eduardo Massera, was sold in 1987 to a private Argentine company. After passing through several owners—including being adapted for anti-hail operations—the aircraft was eventually acquired by a Uruguayan company for use as an air taxi. Since 2008, the plane has remained abandoned in Melilla.

A trial of unprecedented scope in Uruguay, involving crimes committed during the dictatorship and the period of state terrorism, is expected to begin in late 2026. The defendants' counsel repeatedly delayed this proceeding, which should have commenced in 2024. This dilatory tactic is regrettably commonplace in Uruguay.

The case arises from the consolidation, by the Specialized Prosecutor's Office for Crimes against Humanity (headed by prosecutor Ricardo Perciballe), of three independent complaints submitted between October 2020 and May 2021:

- One by Gabriela Schroeder (October 16, 2020), requesting the identification of the material authors of the murders of her mother, Rosario Barredo, and her partner, William Whitelaw. She further petitioned for the investigation of her own abduction and that of her siblings, Victoria and Máximo Whitelaw Barredo, who were, respectively, four years old, 18 months old, and two months old.

- A complaint filed by Benjamín Liberoff (November 4, 2020), seeking answers for the forced disappearance of his father, Manuel Liberoff.
- Relatives of Zelmar Michelini and Héctor Gutiérrez Ruiz initiated a case on May 18, 2021, demanding that those behind their assassinations be held responsible.

To these three petitions was added a resolution of the Inter-American Court of Human Rights (from November 19, 2020), which orders the Uruguayan state to comply with the Gelman v. Uruguay judgment and to investigate the forced disappearance of María Claudia García Iruretagoyena and the suppression of the civil status of Macarena Gelman García. Until now, the case had focused solely on the kidnapping and disappearance of María Claudia, without recognizing Macarena as a direct victim as well.

Prosecutor Perciballe unified the three lawsuits with the Inter-American Court's resolution into a single case. The Prosecutor based this action on the premise that the committed crimes are closely linked and constitute a part of extensive, coordinated actions by various repressive forces that operated illegally and clandestinely in Uruguay and Argentina. As the investigation progressed and the full scale of the atrocities committed in both countries became evident, the initial list of victims expanded significantly, encompassing actions typical of Operation Condor as well as operations that predated the formal establishment of that transnational criminal network. Ultimately, the case covered events from February 1974 to October 1976 because the initially reported episodes were connected to various situations that required a collective assessment for full examination.

Thus, José Arab, Jorge Silveira, Ricardo Medina, Ernesto Ramas, and Gilberto Vázquez were charged with multiple offenses: a dozen homicides, two forced disappearances, two cases of substitution and suppression of the civil status of minors stolen during the dictatorship, and numerous counts of unlawful deprivation of liberty, serious bodily injury, torture, abuse of authority, and robbery. Ramas and Vázquez died before the investigation and the case preparation concluded, so the court cannot try them in this proceeding.

All in all, the trial will be unprecedented in terms of the period covered by the events, the complexity of the crimes under investigation, and the involvement of multiple agents and repressive forces. It will also constitute the first Uruguayan mega-case conducted under the country's new Code of Criminal Procedure, which, among other procedural innovations for the Uruguayan legal system, requires the holding of an oral and public trial.

ACKNOWLEDGMENTS

Our special thanks go to Pincho Casanova and Macarena Montañez, from Pozodeagua, with whom the scripts for the audiovisual pieces Condor on Trial (Memory, Justice and Truth) of the plancondor.org website were developed. The collaborative process of creating these videos was central to shaping the narrative of this book.

We would also like to thank Diego Presa, Mariana Risso, Rodrigo Barbano, Patricia Draper, Javier Cama, Alicia Pérez, Eugenia Sotelo, Federico Tatter, Rosa Palau, Luis Ruiz, Virginia Martínez, Graciela Daleo, Pablo Chargoñia, Observatorio Luz Ibarburu, Sara Méndez, Raúl Olivera, Silvia Ocaña, Ricardo Perciballe, Guillermo Giménez, Fernanda Ramos, Alberto de Austria, Antía Arguiñarena, Lorena Balardini, Melisa Slatman, Pablo Ouviña and his team, Nuria Piñol, Santiago Pedroncini, Clorrie Yeomans, Irini Tseminidou, Diego Sánchez-Ancochea, Chris Williams, Aileen Marshall-Brown, Sam Sneddon, Emma Rundall, and the team of ESCR Impact Acceleration Account of the University of Oxford. Without their contribution and support, this work would not have been possible.

We are deeply grateful to the funders who believed in and supported the Operation Condor project for many years, especially the European Union's Horizon 2020 Research and Innovation Programme under the Marie Marie Skłodowska-Curie grant agreement number 702004, the University of Oxford's ESRC Impact Acceleration Account grants in 2022, and University College London, which, since 2023, is the institutional home of the Plancondor.org project and has helped keep the online platform free and open to all.

We thank Charles Carlini and Casa Carlini Publishing House for believing in this book and making it available to the English-speaking public. We are also very grateful to Alejandro

Reyes for translating the original Spanish book into English and to Alexa-Skye ART for finalising the book proofs. Furthermore, we would like to thank Paulo Slachevsky and Guillermo Bustamento from LOM Ediciones Chile, for letting us the design files of the Chilean edition of the book. Finally, we thank Julián Ubiría, Luisina Ríos, and Gabriela López Introini from Penguin Random House Uruguay for granting us permission to use the book's original design concept.

BIBLIOGRAPHY

Abella, Carlos. El solitario jet de la aviación naval, 2012, https://aerospotter.blogspot.com/2012/09/el-solitario-jet-de-la-aviacion-naval.html

Amado, Cristian. Hawker Siddeley HS-125-400B, LV-AXZ, 2015, https://christianamadospotting.wordpress.com/2015/08/22/hawker-siddeley-hs-125-400b-lv-axz/

Angelucci, Nadia. «Justicia italiana iniciará juicio contra Tróccoli por el asesinato y desaparición de Elena Quinteros y dos argentinos secuestrados en Uruguay», in *La Diaria*, Montevideo, May 5, 2022.

Angelucci Nadia. «Jorge Néstor Tróccoli condenado a cadena perpetua por otros crímenes del Plan Cóndor», in *La Diaria*, Montevideo, October 21, 2025.

Base de Datos sobre los Juicios del Cóndor (1976–2022), June 2023, https://plancondor.org/node/1633

Bertoia, Luciana. El boicot al Mundial 78: Un fracaso que fue todo un éxito, 2010, https://papelitos.com.ar/nota/el-boicot-al-mundial

Blixen, Samuel. *El vientre del Cóndor: Del Archivo del Terror al caso Berríos*, Montevideo: Ediciones de Brecha, 1994.

Brysk, Alison. *The Politics of Human Rights in Argentina*. Stanford, CA: Stanford University Press, 1994.

Calloni, Stella. *Los años del lobo: Operación Cóndor*, Buenos Aires: Ediciones Continente, 2nd ed., 1999.

Calloni, Stella. Los Archivos del Horror del Operativo Cóndor, 1994, https://www.derechos.org/nizkor/doc/condor/calloni.html

Colmán Gutiérrez, Andrés. «Plan Cóndor: Hace 39 años, el avión de la muerte volaba desde Asunción», in *Última Hora*, May 15, 2016, https://www.ultimahora.com/plan-condor-hace-39-anos-el-avion-la-muerte-volaba-asuncion-n991576

Cunha, Luiz Cláudio. *Operación Cóndor: El secuestro de los uruguayos*. Montevideo: Servicio Paz y Justicia, 2017.

Dinges, John. Los años del Cóndor: *Operaciones internacionales de asesinato en el Cono Sur*. Santiago: Debate, 2021.

Dinges, John. *The Condor Years: How Pinochet and His Allies Brought Terrorism to Three Continents.* New York: The New Press, 2005.

Equipo Nizkor. Auto de procesamiento contra Jorge Rafael Videla, 2001, https://www.derechos.org/nizkor/doc/videla1.html

Files of the victims of human rights violations or political violence resulting in death and victims of forced disappearance, qualified by the Truth Commissions in Chile, https://interactivos.museodelamemoria.cl/

Files of victims of kidnapping, forced disappearance, and political assassination in Uruguay (1968–1985), Secretaría de Derechos Humanos para el Pasado Reciente, https://www.gub.uy/secretaria-derechos-humanos-pasado-reciente/victimas

Flecha, Víctor Jacinto. El descubrimiento del Archivo del Terror en 1992, May 28, 2011, https://cultura.gov.py/2011/05/el-descubrimiento-del-archivo-del-terror-en-1992/

Golpe, Alejandro. Hawker Siddeley 125-400, 2013, www.amilarg.com.ar/hawker-125-400.html

González, Mónica. «La historia que no se cuenta de Arancibia Clavel». CIPER, May 1, 2011, https://www.ciperchile.cl/2011/05/01/la-historia-que-no-se-cuenta-de-arancibia-clavel/

IPPDH. *A 40 años del Cóndor: De las coordinaciones represivas a la construcción de las políticas públicas regionales en derechos humanos.* Buenos Aires, Argentina: Instituto de Políticas Públicas en Derechos Humanos del Mercosur, ed. 2015.

«Justicia argentina solicita a Uruguay preservar avión usado en Plan Cóndor», Agence France Press, June 20, 2023.

Kornbluh, Peter. *The Pinochet File: A Declassified Dossier on Atrocity and Accountability.* New York: The New Press, 2013.

Lessa, Francesca. *Los juicios del Cóndor: La coordinación represiva y los crímenes de lesa humanidad en América del Sur.* Montevideo: Taurus/Penguin Random House Uruguay, 2022.

«LV-AXZ (0653 5-T-30), Hawker Siddeley HS-125-400B c/n 25251», Revista Lima Victor, 2016, https://loudandclearisnotenought.blogspot.com/2011/01/lv-axz-hawker-siddeley-hs-125-400b-cn.html

Lessa, Francesca. Los juicios del Cóndor: La coordinación represiva y los crímenes de lesa humanidad en América del Sur. Montevideo: Taurus/Penguin Random House Uruguay, 2022.

Martorell, Francisco. *Operación Cóndor: El vuelo de la muerte.* Santiago: LOM Ediciones, 1999.

McSherry, J. Patrice. *Predatory States: Operation Condor and Covert War in Latin America.* New York: Rowman & Littlefield, 2005.

Meilinger de Sannemann, Gladys. *Paraguay en el Operativo Cóndor: Represión e intercambio clandestino de prisioneros políticos en el Cono Sur.* Asunción, Paraguay: RP Ediciones, 1989.

Ministerio de Justicia y Derechos Humanos de Argentina. «Informe de Investigación sobre Víctimas de Desaparición Forzada y Asesinato, por el accionar represivo del Estado y centros clandestinos de detención y otros lugares de reclusión clandestina», www.argentina.gob.ar/derechoshumanos/ANM/ruvte/informe

Ministerio Público Fiscal Argentina. «Alegato: Plan Cóndor y Automotores Orletti II», 2015, https://www.mpf.gob.ar/plan-condor/alegato/

MMDH, *Operación Cóndor: Historias personales, memorias compartidas.* Santiago: Museo de la Memoria y de los Derechos Humanos, ed. 2015.

Patiño, Nilo y otros. La estructura del poder militar durante la dictadura, https://sitiosdememoria.uy/sites/default/files/2020-01/Estructura.pdf

PIT-CNT. *Desaparecidos: La coordinación represiva.* Montevideo: Secretaría de Derechos Humanos y Políticas Sociales del PIT-CNT, 1998.

Rico, Álvaro. *Investigación histórica sobre detenidos desaparecidos,* 5 Tomos, Montevideo: IMPO, ed. 2007.

Rico, Álvaro. *Investigación histórica sobre dictadura y terrorismo de Estado en el Uruguay (1973-1985),* 3 Tomos, Montevideo: Universidad de la República, ed. 2008.

Romero, Luis Alberto. *Breve Historia Contemporánea de la Argentina.* Fondo de Cultura Económica, 1994.

Federal Penal Oral Court n. 1 of the Federal Capital (Buenos Aires), sentence for lawsuit 1627 entitled «GUILLAMONDEGUI, Néstor Horacio y otros s/privación ilegal de la libertad agravada, imposición de tormentos y homicidio calificado», May 31, 2011 (Orletti I Trial), https://plancondor.org/node/1104

Federal Oral Court n. 1 of the Federal Capital, sentences in lawsuits: 1504, entitled «VIDELA, Jorge Rafael y otros s/privación ilegal de la libertad personal»; 1951, entitled «LOBAIZA, Humberto José Román y otros s/privación ilegal de libertad»; 2054, entitled «FALCÓN, Néstor Horacio y otros s/asociación ilícita y privación ilegal de la libertad»; and 1976, entitled «FURCI, Miguel Ángel s/privación ilegal de la libertad agravada e imposición de tormentos», August 9, 2016 (Operation Cóndor and Orletti II Trials), https://plancondor.org/node/1087

7th Penal Court of Montevideo, Resolution n. 2363 ordering the prosecution with imprisonment of Carlos Calcagno, as a co-author of two crimes of forced disappearance in real concurrence, September 17, 2010, https://plancondor.org/node/1117

Trobo, Claudio. *Asesinato de Estado: ¿quién mató a Michelini y Gutiérrez Ruiz?* Buenos Aires: Ediciones Colihue, 2005.

ABOUT THE AUTHORS

Francesca Lessa is a leading scholar of human rights and state violence in Latin America, driven by a profound commitment to justice and memory. Associate Professor in International Relations of the Americas at University College London, she has spent more than a decade documenting the transnational terror networks behind Operation Condor, blending archival investigation with testimony from survivors and families to illuminate how ordinary people confront extraordinary violence. This book continues the groundbreaking work she first published in Spanish, bringing English-language readers a powerful account shaped by evidence, empathy, and moral clarity. She holds a PhD from the London School of Economics, an MA from SOAS, and a BA from Royal Holloway, University of London.

Sebastián Santana Camargo is an award-winning Uruguayan visual artist, illustrator, and activist whose work often explores themes of memory, state violence, and collective resistance. His striking imagery has accompanied human-rights initiatives across the Southern Cone, bridging visual language with historical truth. In this book, his illustrations serve as a kind of visual testimony, conjuring shadows of the disappeared and echoing the silences that haunt the continent's past. His art does not merely accompany the text; it deepens its emotional resonance and preserves stories that refusal alone could never erase.

www.ingramcontent.com/pod-product-compliance
Ingram Content Group UK Ltd.
Pitfield, Milton Keynes, MK11 3LW, UK
UKHW062310290726
14090UKWH00018B/987